Myths and Practices:

A national survey of the use of experts in child care proceedings

Julia Brophy

Christopher J Wale

Phil Bates

B *r i t i s h*

A *g e n c i e s*

f o r **A** *d o p t i o n*

a n d **F** *o s t e r i n g*

Published by
British Agencies for Adoption & Fostering
(BAAF)
Skyline House
200 Union Street
London SE1 0LX

Registered charity 275689

© BAAF 1999

British Library Cataloguing in Publication Data
A catalogue record for this book is available
from the British Library

ISBN 1 873868 70 7

Editorial project management by Shaila Shah
Designed by Andrew Haig & Associates
Typeset by Avon Dataset Ltd, Bidford on
Avon, Warwickshire B50 4JH
Printed by The Lavenham Press

This work was funded by the Department of
Health and supported by the Lord Chancellor's
Department but the views expressed are those
of the authors alone and do not necessarily
represent those of either Department.

The research was undertaken at the Thomas
Coram Research Unit, Institute of Education,
University of London.

Contents

Acknowledgments

This research project is funded by the Department of Health and supported by the Lord Chancellor's Department. We are grateful to Carolyn Davies, Senior Principal Research Officer, Research and Development Division and Arran Poyser, Social Services Inspector, Department of Health, for their continued support.

We have benefitted enormously from the support and advice of the project's Advisory Committee: Gresham Chown (Chair, National Association of Guardians *ad litem* and Reporting Officers, from April 1995 to October 1995), Katherine Gieve (Solicitor, Bindman and Partners), Susan Golombok (Director, Clinical and Health Psychology Research Unit, City University), Jean Harris Hendriks (Consultant in Child and Adolescent Psychiatry), Joan Jarvis (Guardian *ad litem* and Reporting Officer, Inner and North London Panel), Mavis Maclean (Senior Research Fellow, Centre for Socio-Legal Studies, Wolfson College, Oxford), Panna Modi (Guardian ad Litem and Reporting Officer for the Leicester panel, Consultant to the Nottingham panel and Independent Assessor for the Birmingham panel and Project Manager – Child Care, at the National Society for the Prevention of Cruelty to Children, Leicester), Neville Paul (Family Policy Division, Lord Chancellor's Department), Mary Ryan (Co-Director, Family Rights Group), Jill Woodhead (Chair, National Association of Guardians *ad litem* and Reporting Officers, from March 1994 to April 1995) and to Sue Cooper (Chair April 1995 to date). In particular, we are especially grateful to the Chair of that Committee, Joyce Plotnikoff, Guardian *ad litem* and Independent Consultant in civil and criminal justice, for her work on that committee and for her comments. We have used this Committee mercilessly and we are extremely grateful for their time and energy.

This study could not have progressed without the enormous help and continued support of the GALRO service. Firstly, we are especially indebted to the panel managers and guardians who were involved in pilot work during stage I of the study. In particular we wish to thank Nancy Drucker (Panel Manager for Oxford) and the Oxford Panel of Guardians, Pam Thomas (Panel Manager for Bedford) and the Bedford Panel of Guardians, Patricia Walton (Panel Manager for Cheshire) and the Cheshire Panel of Guardians and Richard Holden (Panel Manager for South London during 1993) and the South London Panel of Guardians. In addition we would like to thank Adrian Grocott (Panel Manager for Essex) and the Essex Panel of Guardians.

Secondly, we wish to thank the 34 panel managers and their administrators for the enormous help we received in locating the target sample of guardians for the main study. Thirdly, we wish to thank the 338 guardians themselves who completed and returned the final schedule. They completed a lengthy questionnaire in their own time and during a period when concerns about payment issues remain high on their agenda. Nevertheless, a response rate of 71 per cent is illustrative of their commitment to the issues and the development of the service. We are indebted to them both for their time and the additional comments and suggestions many of them made.

We are also heavily indebted to Sheila Field and Vivienne Metliss (administrative assistants on the GALRO project) for their unstinting and professional work. Finally, our thanks to colleagues at Thomas Coram Research Unit (TCRU), in particular, June Statham, Tony Munton and Ann Mooney. Particular thanks are due to Charlie Owen for considerable technical assistance on questionnaire design, computing support and data entry and also to Ian Plewis for advice on the survey sampling technique and statistical support.

Foreword

This empirical study is the first to examine the role of the expert in care proceedings following the implementation of the Children Act 1989. It brings to light a number of challenging issues for the administration of the family justice system and its relationship with health and social services. A basic dilemma is that the more sophisticated the machinery of family justice becomes, the more elaborate and slower the process.

Guardians *ad litem* now play a pivotal role in the conduct of these proceedings, not only representing the child but selecting various experts and advising the courts as to time tabling. The study confirms that we are witnessing a growth in the use of specialist medical experts – paediatricians, child psychiatrists, psychologists and so forth – and considers the reasons for it, including doubts about relying on social work assessments alone. The adversarial nature of proceedings can result in each disputing party engaging his or her own expert, upon which it becomes a progressively more difficult administrative task to arrange matters so that all the medical specialists and all the parties and witnesses are present at the trial. The more practitioners there are the more complex the collaborative task.

A central problem concerns the availability of certain specialists, a number of whom can be reluctant to get entangled in care proceedings, because of competing priorities such as clinics. Moreover from time to time their expert opinions conflict, particularly in the mental health field if they represent different schools of thought, adding to the dispute element in the litigation. Also the pool of available consultants is determined in part by the willingness of their employers to permit them to undertake court related duties, a particular problem for health service consultants. There is thus a danger of limiting the range of experience and expertise available to the courts. Justice is not served if that pool is too limited and esoteric.

In all this one has to ask whose interests are paramount – the child (as legislation intends) or the practitioners and administrators of the system? Julia Brophy and her colleagues highlight once again, as others have done, the enduring problem of delay, normally to be regarded as detrimental to the welfare of the child. It is thus disturbing to learn (see Table 4.10) that, of 540 cases sampled, 42 per cent lasted longer than eight months. As 50 per cent of the sample were less than four years old, one can only wonder what iatrogenic harm was done during this interim period to the children's attachments and education, particularly to those who may have experienced a series of short-term moves. It was the judgement of the guardians *ad litem* that in a third of the cases delays in getting expert assessments completed on time prejudiced the child's interests.

Another contributing element relating to delay, as the study shows, is the decision to transfer cases to higher courts. Part of the problem is that much court case management is weak. In this respect it is extraordinary how slow the government's judicial administration has been to apply information technology, particularly in measuring case flows through the system. Thus the authors have done a public service in drawing attention to the need for courts to set target deadlines and to determine case by case a maximum acceptable waiting period. Clearly guardians *ad litem* are going to have to be more robust about this than they have in the past.

The great merit of research like this is that it brings the facts to light and exposes the gap between aspirational legislative and professional rhetoric and the day-to-day realities of interprofessional practice. Until this research the truth was that, with respect to the use of experts in family courts, nobody knew what was happening and therefore very few cared. I hope that all who read this excellent study (and related publications) will re-double their efforts to overcome all the systemic weaknesses here exposed. Failure to do so will amount to a disturbingly complacent willingness to tolerate poor interprofessional practice and maladministration of justice. The main victims will be the never-ending stream of disadvantaged children and parents that creep through the courts, mostly uncomplainingly through ignorance or fear of doing otherwise.

Mervyn Murch
Professor in Law
Cardiff Law School
Cardiff University
March 1999

Introduction

The guardian *ad litem* and the court

The guardian *ad litem* in care proceedings is an independent social worker who is appointed by the court to represent and safeguard the interests of children in public law proceedings. The guardian *ad litem* also has a duty to represent the interests of the child and to act as an adviser to the court. His or her powers and duties are set out in the Children Act 1989 and in two sets of Rules.* The Children Act 1989 extended the role of the guardian and increased its importance. Thus, guardians will usually be appointed in all public law proceedings and are now required to advise the court on a range of issues including allocation of cases to the appropriate court, the timetabling of cases, the use of experts and how to keep delays in the processing of cases to a minimum. When guardians were first introduced to care proceedings in 1984, local authorities were required to establish panels of guardians.

In their role as the representative of children, the guardian has a major responsibility for both identifying the wishes and feelings of children and advising the court as to what is in the child's best interests. Thus the guardian plays a critical role when important decisions are being made by professionals and courts about a child's future. He or she can therefore both seek leave (i.e. permission) of the court to appoint expertise beyond those of social work to provide additional information for the court, and can advise the court on the necessity of experts proposed by other parties to proceedings (i.e. the local authority, the child's parents, grandparents and other potential carers).

Directions appointment/hearings have been introduced to maintain the court's control over proceedings and deal with procedural issues to ensure the case is ready to be heard at the final hearing. Such hearings are now held in all tiers of the court structure and it is at those hearings that the guardian is expected to play a crucial role in advising the court on the preparation of the case and on any further assessments which may be necessary. One of the central tasks of directions hearings is to draw up a timetable for cases and thus try to avoid delay as required by section 1(2) of the Children Act.

The project

The project from which this study is drawn is entitled "The Guardians *ad Litem*, Expert Evidence and Child Care Proceedings Project". It contains four separate but related studies. In addition to this survey, Stage I of the project included a court-based study (Bates & Brophy, forthcoming), Stage II of the project focused on the views and practices of guardians in three different geographical locations (Brophy & Bates, 1999), and Stage III examines the views and experiences of a group of experts in the field of child and adolescent psychiatry.

Although there was considerable concern surrounding the involvement of experts in care and related proceedings following the Children Act 1989, there are a number of problems in examining the use of experts in any systematic way. Not only was there an absence of national data on these issues in the period prior to the 1989 Act but, moreover, following the Act, there was still no way of ascertaining from government statistics how many

* The Family Proceedings Rules 1991, part IV and, The Family Proceedings Courts (Children Act 1989) Rules 1991.

cases involved experts, what types of experts were being used in proceedings and how available/willing experts were to undertake work in the context of court proceedings.

Pilot interviews had suggested an increase in the use of experts and that work also indicated a level of concern amongst both guardians and experts about a number of practices emerging in this area of public law. Guardians, for example, expressed concern about both the availability and willingness of experts to accept the growing number of instructions from parties – a concern also expressed by some experts. Equally, the approach of guardians to the use of experts appeared to be changing. Although the reasons underlying this change appear to be quite complex, the practices of local authorities and perceptions of local court "cultures" were implicated in discussions about how the nature of the legal process was changing.

The issues and aims of the survey

The aim of the survey was to address two main areas.* First, in the absence of national data on the use of experts in care proceedings, we aimed to address some broad questions about levels of use of experts, their availability and guardians' satisfaction with services provided. Second, we aimed to examine some specific questions about the practices employed by various professionals during the course of legal proceedings.

The survey was therefore divided into two main sections. Section I focused on identifying levels of use, including the reasons why there has been an increase in the use of experts in public law proceedings, levels of satisfaction with local child and adolescent mental health services, the impact of a shortage of experts, and the criteria used by guardians when appointing certain child health and development specialists. In Section I we also looked at whether panel managers provided any assistance to guardians in finding appropriate experts.

Section II focused on a sample of 557 completed cases involving experts and addressed a range of questions about the practices of local authorities, courts and guardians. We examined the profile of cases involving experts (e.g. the age and number of children involved in proceedings, the types of applications made and the outcomes, the courts which made the final order, and the length of cases). We identified the parties responsible for the expert reports filed, and the dominant disciplines being used by parties.

In the case of sole instructions to experts, we examined consultation practices where either guardians or local authorities were the only party to instruct experts and file reports. We also examined the role of the court in such cases and whether attempts were made to encourage parties to seek joint letters of instruction. We addressed the issue of delay and whether (in the case of sole instructions) the use of experts had led to delay in cases.

We also examined cases where more than one party had filed expert evidence (potentially the most complex and lengthy cases). We asked guardians to identify whether more than one expert had addressed the same issues or concerns within a case, the reasons why second opinions had been sought, and the impact of that process on the child or children involved. We also compared some aspects of the resultant reports.

* The survey also contained a section on training issues in the guardian service and this has been reported elsewhere (Brophy, Wale & Bates (1997) *Training and Support: The Guardian ad Litem and Reporting Officer Service*, DOH/Welsh Office/TCRU

The experts commissioned and the relevant proceedings

The types of experts included in the questionnaire were drawn from the disciplines identified during interviews in the pilot stage of the project and in the court-based study (Bates & Brophy, forthcoming, see Table 23). In most cases the expert reports filed were from paediatricians, psychiatrists and, to a lesser extent, psychologists focusing on the child and/or adults in the proceedings. However, we also asked guardians to include reports from advisers on ethnicity issues and also independent social work reports (e.g. reports from family centres on parenting skills assessments) where such reports were filed within proceedings.

We asked guardians to include **all expert reports filed in cases** (i.e. those based on assessments which predated proceedings but which were filed within proceedings, those reports which involved direct contact with or observation of children and adults, and those which were based on a "paper assessment").

For the purposes of this survey we asked guardians to focus on applications for care and supervision orders, discharge/variation of care or supervision orders, extension of supervision orders and applications for contact with a child in care, or permission to refuse contact with such a child. We refer to these as "care and related" proceedings. We excluded child assessment orders, secure accommodation orders and change of name or an application for a child to be taken out of the country.

The sample size and methodology

When the project began there were 56 Guardian *ad Litem* and Reporting Officer panels in England and Wales.* In the period immediately following the Children Act 1989, there was no reliable information on the total number of guardians (some put the figure at 2,000 while others suggested it was as low as 1,500). Published figures are based on registrations (not people) and contain no information with regard to levels of activity within the registered workforce. The initial aim was to produce a sample of approximately 500 active guardians. Panels were stratified according to membership size and panels were then randomly selected from this frame. This produced a sample of 36 panels with a total of 721 registrations.

Following consultations with panel managers and members, membership lists were screened to eliminate dual registrations and, because the focus of the survey was on experts in care and related proceedings, panel members who undertook adoption cases (ie: reporting officers and adoption-only guardians) were also excluded. Equally, guardians who were registered with panels but who, in practice, had not taken any cases since implementation of the Children Act 1989 were also excluded. One panel was excluded because it was undergoing considerable change and was without a panel manager in post; a consortium[†] was established during the period between the initial contact and the distribution of the questionnaire, thus reducing the sample size by one further panel. With regard to panels, therefore, the final sample consisted of 34 participating panels, comprising 476 guardians who were eligible to participate.

The group of 476 of guardians were sent copies of the questionnaire in January 1995. The reminder and follow-up procedure was a three stage process: the first reminder letter and a further copy of the questionnaire for non-respondents, followed by a second reminder letter, followed by a telephone call each at approximately 15-day intervals. A total of 338 questionnaires were returned. The response rate was therefore 71 per cent.

* The number of panels now stands at 59 (54 in England and 5 in Wales) (DoH, 1995).

† Most GALRO panels are single authority panels, but a number of authorities have entered into consortium arrangements to provide the service. For example, the Inner and North London GALRO Service is administered by the National Children's Bureau on behalf of 26 London boroughs.

We estimate this sample of guardians represents approximately 44 per cent of the workforce.*

The majority of the questions in the questionnaire were followed by closed or "forced-choice" response options. The options available were drawn from pilot work with (in total) four panels† and the policy issues outlined in the above introduction – but with the option of "other response" if the guardian felt their views/experiences fell outside of the range of responses contained in the questionnaire. There were, in addition, a limited number of open-ended questions and the themes arising from those responses are based on a sub-sample of 55 schedules.

With regard to Section II of the schedule which focused on some substantive issues and practices of the professionals, we asked guardians to provide detailed information on the profile of their two most recently completed cases which had involved experts. We then asked a range of questions (mostly "forced-choice") about their own practices and those of the local authorities and courts involved in those cases.

A profile of the guardians in the survey

The majority of the guardians in the survey are members of one panel only (70 per cent) and half the sample had been working for their current panel for *at least* six years. Most were freelance** (79 per cent), and most freelance guardians (62 per cent) work on a part-time or on an occasional basis. The sample was predominantly female (76 per cent) and white European (94 per cent). Many guardians had considerable previous experience as social workers prior to their first appointment as a guardian – 50 per cent had *at least* 15 years previous experience in social work (although, of course, not all previous experience was necessarily based in what is now termed child protection work/teams).

Almost all the guardians in the survey had undergone induction training; 37 per cent of the sample had also completed or were undertaking post-qualifying studies leading to a further qualification or higher degree relevant to their work as a guardian. A high proportion of guardians continued to attend further training events following their induction training with panels. During 1994 (the year preceding the survey), 89 per cent of guardians had attended panel-organised training events and almost two-thirds had attended at least two additional events hosted by other organisations. The training profile of the guardians in the survey is examined in detail elsewhere (Brophy, Wale & Bates, 1997).

* As we outline above, it has been difficult to estimate the total number of guardians at any one time because a number of freelance guardians are registered with more than one panel and, since available figures are based on registrations, this inevitably leads to some double counting (hence the difficulty of estimating the total workforce at the start of the survey). Our estimates are based on the published figures for panel memberships (DoH, 1994) (excluding Probation) which gives *registrations* as 1,045. As outlined above, our sample was screened to eliminate dual registrations. The 338 guardians who responded to the survey represented 462 registrations. Thus we estimate that our sample of 338 respondents represented 44 per cent of the workforce in 1994.

† The range of set options of responses were developed on the basis of the following pilot work: telephone interviews with 14 members of one (single authority) panel of guardians plus an analysis of a sample of panel records followed by a group discussion with panel members. This was followed by semi-structured interviews lasting approximately two hours with six members of a consortium panel in a different geographical location. A draft questionnaire was then constructed which consisted of questions followed by a list of set option responses; a limited number of open-ended questions were also included. A postal questionnaire was then piloted with all members of a further single authority panel plus selected members of an additional panel.

** Guardians in this employment category have been variously referred to as self-employed, "fee attracting sessional workers" and "fee attractors". In all cases they are self-employed social workers appointed by panels to work as guardians on a fees-based contract. For ease of presentation in this and other publications from the project they are referred to throughout as freelance guardians.

The use of experts in child care proceedings following the Children Act 1989

Despite the absence of national data on how much expert evidence is filed in care and related cases, writers and clinicians have expressed concern about both a perceived increase in usage and the impact which the use of experts might have on delay in public law cases (eg: CAAC, 1994/5; Wolkind, 1994; Plotnikoff & Woolfson, 1994). We therefore began by asking guardians to focus on their case load for the year January – December 1994 and

- estimate the percentage of their cases which involved experts (commissioned by any party)
- indicate whether they had experienced an increase in the use of experts since the Children Act and which parties they thought had increased their use
- indicate if they had increased their *own* use of experts and the reasons for that change in practice.

a)   How often are experts involved?

The survey identified a relatively high use of experts. For the calendar year 1994, over half the sample (56 per cent) estimated that *at least* 40 per cent of their case load involved expert evidence. Over a quarter of the sample (29 per cent) estimated that *at least* 60 per cent of their case load involved experts (see Table 2.1).

	Full-time %	Part-time or occasional* %	All guardians %
None	2	4	3
Less than 10%	10	20	16
10 – 39%	28	24	25
40 – 60%	34	22	27
61 – 75%	13	11	12
More than 75%	13	19	17
Total	100	100	100

Table 2.1

Estimated percentage of case load (care and related proceedings) which involved experts by hours worked for year 1994

Note: * 62% of the sample workforce work part-time or work on an occcasional basis.
N = 134 (full-time)
N = 189 (part-time)
(missing – 5)

b)   Has there been an increase in the use of experts and, if so, which party or parties have increased their use?

Of those guardians who had both pre- and post- Children Act experience on their current panels, 88 per cent said that there had been an increase in the use of experts since the introduction of the Children Act.

Not surprisingly, responsibility for that increase does not appear to rest with one party in proceedings:

- 89 per cent of respondents indicated local authorities were increasing their use
- 90 per cent said guardians were increasing their use
- 88 per cent said parents were increasing their use.

For those guardians who had both pre- and post- Children Act experience on their current panel, 70 per cent stated that they had increased their *own* use of experts since the Act.

Leaving aside for the moment the question of whether this development in legal proceedings represents a positive change for the children and families concerned, the reasons underlying changes in professional practices are clearly complex. There have been some substantial changes to law and legal procedures, for example, the new "threshold" criteria and the focus on contact and care plans, the move from oral to written evidence, and the loss of professional legal privilege (and thus the requirement that all expert evidence is filed whether or not it is favourable to the instructing party). Some guardians in the pilot work suggested the practices of local authorities (in both social services and legal services departments) had changed with regard to establishing "proof" (the threshold criteria) and the need for a court order and local authorities were using experts to add weight to or to confirm existing views. Equally there was a suggestion that some local authorities were trying to save funds by asking guardians to appoint experts and thus fund the commission from the legal aid fund.

Also relevant are practices in case management by guardians,* and linked to the practices of both guardians and local authorities are expectations of local court "cultures" with regard to the use of experts. There was, for example, a limited suggestion in the pilot survey that some judges were reluctant to remove children except on the say-so of a psychiatrist.

Perhaps equally important in understanding this apparent shift in practice are the responses of parents themselves, their advocates and support groups for parents[†] to the increasing body of expertise seen to be mounted against them.

In addition, the arrangements for funding the work of expert witnesses, and the relatively easier/quicker access to funding available to guardians compared with some local authorities, clearly overlap these legal and institutional changes adding further complexity to a picture which is already geographically quite diverse.

Some of these issues require a more detailed investigation than is possible in a postal survey. These were pursued in stages II and III of the study. Nevertheless, there are some "base line" questions about the trends in practices of all parties which can be addressed in a survey.

For example, in the early period following the Children Act, the Expert Witness Group suggested that perhaps the increase in the use of experts might be due to local authorities looking to other parties to provide evidence which traditionally, they, (as the applicant) have provided.** Guardians in the pilot interviews gave some examples of local authority practices which added some weight to that view.

Moreover, some guardians in the pilot survey expressed concern about the undervaluing of social work expertise both by social workers themselves and also by courts and the consequent pressures to have some decisions "authenticated" by experts. In the guardian service, for example, at training

* There was some anecdotal suggestion of overuse of experts by guardians at the time of the survey. However, shortly after its completion, there was *also* a suggestion that guardians were in fact reluctant to appoint experts in appropriate cases (see Wall, 1995).

† For example, The Family Rights Group (FRG).

** The Expert Witness Group was a working party of various professional bodies and individuals from both academic and clinical practice in law, medicine, social work, psychiatry and psychology. The Group examined a range of issues about the use of experts in civil proceedings, including the provision of a curriculum vitae for expert witnesses, and proposals for this were approved by the Children Act Advisory Committee. See CAAC *Annual Report 1992/3*; Annex 1, pp 24/25.

workshops and seminars* concern has also been expressed that perhaps some guardians were not doing as much as they could to stem an overuse or misuse of experts, and were perhaps using experts to undertake work which they or social workers could/should undertake.

For those guardians who had experienced an increase in the use of experts and who said they had increased their *own* use, we sought to identify whether issues identified in certain geographical areas during the pilot study were indicative of more general trends.

c) Why are guardians increasing their use of experts?

We asked those (70 per cent) guardians who said they had increased their own use of experts to identify the reasons underlying this change in practice. We begin below by first addressing some of the justifications in common currency in this field and Table 2.2 dispels some popular myths about the practices of guardians with regard to their use of experts:

- Only two per cent of guardians said they used experts to cut down on their time in complex cases.

- Despite concerns over pay issues in the profession and the large differentials in the fees paid to guardians as compared with those paid to other specialists/experts, only two per cent said this was one reason for their increased use of experts.

- Less than a quarter of the sample (21 per cent) identified that the "spiral" effect (initiated by the local authority's use of experts) was in part responsible for their own increased use of experts.

Some of the popular views about court pressures to use experts are also dispelled:

- Few guardians (11 per cent) said they had increased their use of experts

Reasons	%
Local authority practices:	
Local authorities are using them more and it's a "spiral"	21
Local authorities are relying on the guardian to provide essential evidence	41
Better 'access' issues:	
Guardian has a wider choice of experts / is not so constrained in choice as local authority	60
Guardian has quicker/easier access to funding than the local authority	44
Court "expectations":	
When other parties have experts, courts expect the guardian to have one	9
Courts do not value social work expertise and guardians therefore need the backing and status of an expert	41
Courts are unwilling to remove children unless a psychiatrist says so	11
Guardian's own practices:	
Guardian has a heavy case load and it cuts down time in complex cases	2
Experts are paid more for assessments and for the pressures	1
Cases demand a diagnosis of mental health states	57
Complexity of cases	92

Table 2.2

Reasons why guardians have increased their use of experts

Note: N = 169 (based on guardians who said they had increased their own use)

* e.g. Group Feedback, *Practice in Progress (1994) – The A-Z of Case Management*, National Report from Four Regional Conferences for Guardians *ad Litem* and Reporting Officers, IRCHIN/DoH.

because courts were unwilling to remove children unless a psychiatrist supported that decision.

• Less than 10 per cent said courts expected the guardian to have an expert if experts were commissioned by other parties in proceedings.

However, some of the concerns about the undervaluing of social work expertise by courts have contributed to guardians' increased use of experts:

• 41 per cent said that courts did not value social work expertise and therefore guardians needed the backing and status of an expert.

Policies and practices adopted by some local authorities have also contributed to the increased use of experts by some guardians:

• 41 per cent said that local authorities were relying on guardians to provide essential evidence.

• 60 per cent said the fact that they were not as constrained as the local authority in their choice of expert was a reason why their use of experts had increased.

• 44 per cent said their easier and quicker access to funding for expert assessments was part of the reason for their own increased use of experts.

With regard to parenting, children and mental health issues:

• Over half the sample (57 per cent) said they had increased their use of experts because cases demanded a diagnosis of a mental health state.

With regard to the increased complexity of cases and the use of experts:

• Almost all (92 per cent) also identified "complexity" of cases as a reason why they had increased their own use of experts.

The notion of "complexity" in this field of law is difficult to "unpack". Complexity within a case is of course one reason for transferring it to a higher court (e.g. from the family proceedings courts to a care centre). However, it is usually one of a number of reasons for transfer and is frequently combined with the existence of conflicting expert evidence within a case and hence, the anticipated length of the final hearing (Bates & Brophy, forthcoming).

Moreover, it is also arguable that all families are complex since human behaviour is highly variable, and family breakdown and failures in parenting are also complex, and research on the backgrounds of children who enter local authority care suggests there are a number of social and economic factors contributing to that situation (Bebbington & Miles, 1989).* It is doubtful if family structures and parenting behaviours, styles and practices are substantially more problematic or complex in the early 1990s than they were in the decade prior to the 1989 Children Act, although there are some indications that more children are living in poverty. However, the child protection system and the legal threshold at which those behaviours are judged, and the ideologies underlying the perceived relationship between the family and the state have changed.†

In a closed choice question, therefore, we asked guardians to consider some of the legal changes (hypothesised by Plotnikoff & Woolfson, 1994) in the

* For example, Bebbington and Miles building on the work of previous researchers such as Packman (1968; 1986) identify risk factors such as coming from broken families, living in poor (and overcrowded) housing conditions, with a parent in receipt of (what was) supplementary benefit, being of mixed ethnic "origin", having a mother under 21, coming from a large family (four or more children) and living in a poor neighbourhood, and examine the effect of each factor and the probability of admission into care.

† A range of changes have been introduced aimed at rebalancing the relationship between families and the state, for example, the movement towards preventative work and a recognition of the need for social services to work in partnership with parents in the care of children (*Working Together*, 1989).

context of what they perceived as increased "complexity" in their case load (see Table 2.3). Two issues dominated explanations of the increased complexity of cases. The first relates to the types of cases which guardians have undertaken since the Act. The second focuses on the impact of the provisions of the Children Act itself:

- Most guardians (62 per cent) indicated that one of the reasons why they thought their cases were more complex (and why they had therefore increased their use of experts) was that they were taking cases which, prior to the Children Act, would have been dealt with under wardship proceedings. In effect, they considered they were representing children in an arguably more serious category of work.*

- 58 per cent indicated that the need to determine whether the local authority's care plan was in a child's best interests† also increased "complexity", and hence, increased their use of experts.

- 54 per cent identified the new legal threshold criteria – the need to determine whether the child is suffering or is likely to suffer significant harm – as making cases more complex.**

- 53 per cent indicated that the need to determine questions of contact†† increased the complexity of cases, and hence, increased their use of experts.

Reasons	%
Previously these cases would have been dealt with under Wardship Proceedings	62
The need to determine whether the local authority care plan is in the child's best interests	58
The need to determine whether the child is suffering or is likely to suffer Significant harm	54
The need to consider questions of contact at the time when the Court Order is made	53
Other reasons	37

Table 2.3

Reasons why guardians consider cases are more complex

Note: N = 156 (based on those guardians who identified 'complexity' as a reason why they had increased their own use of experts)

Summary

- **How often are experts involved?**
  A relatively high percentage of guardians' cases in care proceedings during the year 1994 involved experts – over half of the sample said *at least* 40 per cent of their cases involved experts, over a quarter said *at least* 60 per cent of the cases involved experts.

- **Which parties have increased their use of experts?**
  All parties have increased their use of experts in care and related proceedings.

- **Have guardians also increased their use of experts?**
  Most guardians have increased their own use of experts. Several issues underscored this change of practice:

  - *Changes to law and legal procedure*
    Almost all guardians said cases are more complex because of the increased range of issues to be considered when a court order is sought: the new legal threshold, questions of future parental contact

* But see, Hunt (1993) *Local Authority Wardships before the Children Act: The baby or the bathwater?*

† See DoH (1991c) *The Children Act 1989 Guidance and Regulations, Vol 3, Family Placements*, p.15. para 2.62.

** Children Act 1989 s.31 (2)(a)(b). Prior to the new criteria under the Children Act, under the Children and Young Persons Act 1969, s.1, the court had power to make orders if satisfied that: *any person under seventeen who is not married is (a) in need of care and control which he is unlikely to receive unless the court makes an order, and (b) that any one of the following conditions is fulfilled: (I) His proper development is being avoidably prevented or neglected, his health is being avoidably impaired or neglected or he is being ill-treated. (ii) It is probable that the condition set out [above] will be satisfied in his case, having regard to the fact that the court or another court has found that condition is or was satisfied in the case of another child or young person who is or was a member of the household to which he belongs. (iii) He is exposed to moral danger. (iv) He is beyond the control of his parent or guardian. (v) He is of compulsory school age within the meaning of the Education Act 1944 and is not receiving efficient full-time education suitable to his age, ability and aptitude. (vi) He is guilty of an offence, excluding homicide.*

†† Children Act 1989 s.34 (a)(b)(d)

and the need to determine whether the care plan is in the child's best interests.

The loss of wardship proceedings was also seen as contributing to the increased use of experts.

- *Existence of mental health concerns*
  Although over half the sample identified that cases demanded a diagnosis of a mental health state, nevertheless, a substantial proportion did not identify mental health issues as one of the reasons underlying their own increased use of experts.

- *Policies and practices of local authorities*
  Most of the sample identified that the limited pool of experts on which local authorities could draw had an impact on their own use of experts – guardians are not as geographically constrained as some local authorities are in their choice of experts and can appoint from outside of the local area.

  A substantial group also identified the fact that they could obtain quicker/easier funding than the local authority as a reason why their use had increased.

- *Undervaluing of social work skills*
  A substantial group identified that the undervaluing of social work skills and expertise by courts also contributed to their increased use of experts in 1994.

- *Proliferation of experts?*
  Contrary to popular debate, guardians in this survey did not identify the "spiral" (or "domino") effect as a major reason why they have increased their own use of experts.

- *Pressures of work and pay differentials*
  Guardians did not indicate heavy case loads or pay differentials as reasons why they had increased their use of experts to undertake assessments they themselves might otherwise undertake.

Child and adolescent mental health services

3

Introduction

There are a number of concerns about the provision of child and adolescent mental health services in the context of legal proceedings. For example, the court-based study conducted as part of this project (Bates & Brophy, forthcoming) identified that in one geographical location, overall, child and adolescent psychiatrists were the major providers of expert assessments and reports for courts. However, such experts were seldom appointed from local services (i.e within the local authority area). Hence, children and families often travelled a considerable distance to the mental health experts commissioned by the local authority or the guardians to participate in what were variously termed "psychiatric assessments" or "family psychiatric assessments" (Brophy & Bates, 1998).

Moreover, in pilot interviews some guardians expressed a range of concerns about the willingness and availability of specialists in local services to undertake assessments and about the quality of some of this work. Experts themselves have expressed concerns about the changing nature of child and adolescent mental health services, the limited resources available within such services, and the way in which assessments and reports for court proceedings stretched already severely limited resources (Trowell, 1991; Sepping, 1992; Wolkind, 1993).

In beginning to address the relationship between "demand" and "supply" (i.e. the needs of parties for expert assessments and the ability of specialists in child and adolescent mental health services to provide a service at an appropriate level of expertise) we asked guardians:

- whether they were satisfied with local services;

- what improvements were required; and

- what criteria they used when appointing experts in the field of child psychiatry and psychology.

We then explored the question of the shortage of experts and asked:

- how serious this issue was and if it had resulted in many failures to appoint;

- whether expertise in some disciplines was more difficult to obtain than others;

- about reluctance of some specialists to undertake court work and possible explanations for this;

- whether panel managers or committees provided any assistance in locating appropriate experts.

a) Satisfaction with local services

Relatively few guardians were satisfied with local services in the field of child and adolescent mental health:

- 19 per cent were mostly satisfied;

- 31 per cent were not satisfied; and

- 50 per cent said it was variable and depended on the area.

We asked guardians to identify the problems they had experienced with local services:

- 72 per cent stated that local services had no resources or commitment to undertake further therapeutic work if it was necessary;

- 63 per cent said services lacked staff with experience in undertaking assessments and preparing reports for courts;

- 59 per cent had experienced delays in getting reports from experts; and

- 49 per cent said that the assessments undertaken were not sufficiently thorough.

b) Improvements required to local child and adolescent mental health services

In an open-ended question, we asked guardians to identify the improvements they wished to see in local services. As Table 3.1 highlights, themes emerging from a limited analysis of responses to this question focused on resources and training issues and the need to involve a number of professionals in a multidisciplinary exercise.

Table 3.1

Improvements required to services

Based on a random sub-sample of 55 responses to an open-ended question

Improvements required
More locally based services able to offer ongoing help
More resources, therefore more staff
Better trained, more experienced staff
Multidisciplinary teams able to offer a wider range of expertise

c) What do guardians look for in an expert?

Addressing the criteria which guardians apply when seeking to appoint a particular specialist is a complex exercise. This task is made more problematic because there is a gap between demands for expert assessments and the availability of suitably trained specialists. Hence, in practice, it is likely that appointments will increasingly be made on the basis of who is available and willing rather than who is necessarily the best or most appropriate expert to undertake a given assessment.

Despite that problem it is nevertheless important to address the question of the criteria used in selecting experts. First, it has implications for the development of services and for the training of future and current specialists within those services. It is thus important to identify what is required of specialists and services if they are to respond effectively and make a real contribution to improving decision making with regard to the future care and upbringing of children and families at risk.

Second, interviews in the pilot stages indicated a range of judgements were being made according to a "taken for granted" logic amongst guardians. For example, guardians in one panel indicated that even though it was getting extremely difficult to instruct their first choice, they were almost unanimous in their resistance to instructing someone they or their panel colleagues had not instructed previously.

In another panel, some guardians indicated they had to go further afield to obtain expert assessments and some expressed anxieties about an increasing gap between who they would like to appoint, and who they actually appointed. Going further afield not only means children and families may have further to travel, it may also mean guardians are having to make judgements about people with no firsthand knowledge of their work or experience in this field. It may also mean those experts then become less available to *their* local catchment area. It also raises issues about the location of and responsibility for any further therapeutic work which might be necessary for the children and families.

Addressing the criteria by which guardians appoint experts is also made difficult by a further factor which underlies and indeed underscores good social work practice. Each case (each child and each parent) is different, the dynamics of each family are different, and the concerns which have to be addressed and the needs of the particular child or children will differ. Thus, the ethos which informs good social work practice identifies the importance of the individual as the starting point. Therefore, asking guardians to reflect on how decisions are made about who to instruct, or what influences decision making in the absence of a specific case (i.e in the abstract), is not an exercise which fits easily within the dominant ethos of the profession.

There are nevertheless some overriding concerns about the use of experts in the legal arena which we sought to address. Some of these arose from the pilot work and some emerged from contemporary debates in this field.* Therefore, accepting that the needs of each child and each parent *are* different, we asked guardians to indicate (from a list of options) what *other* factors are important in determining their choice of: first, a child and adolescent psychiatrist and second, a child psychologist.

Table 3.2 demonstrates that two major themes underscored the criteria for appointing child psychiatrists. First, they must be known to be sensitive to the *particular* needs and concerns of children and families who are the subject of care proceedings. Second, guardians want a *known and experienced expert witness:*

- 84 per cent said they wanted someone known to be sensitive to the particular needs and concerns of children and families in public law proceedings;

- 74 per cent said they wanted someone they had used before and whose judgement they trusted;

- 73 per cent wanted someone *experienced in court work who could withstand cross examination* (emphasis added); and

- 71 per cent also identified they wanted someone who produces reports for courts which clearly distinguish "fact and opinion".

Where guardians seek to appoint a psychologist to undertake an assessment of a child, as Table 3.3 demonstrates, two themes dominate the criteria for

* For example, from the work of King & Piper, 1990; King, 1991: King & Trowell, 1992; James, 1992.

Determining factors	%
Someone sensitive to needs of families	84
Someone I have used before and whose judgement I trust	74
Someone experienced in court work who can withstand cross-examination	73
Someone who produces reports which distinguish between fact and opinion	71
Someone with proven ability to report to specified time scales	63
Someone with a willingness to undertake further therapeutic work	52
Someone whose reports include research	38
Someone who is locally based	33
Someone who is part of a multidisciplinary team	31
It's a matter of "trial and error"	8
Obtaining the most senior consultant	7

Table 3.2

Important factors determining choice of a child and adolescent psychiatrist to undertake a child/ family assessment

Note: N = 331

appointment. First, they wanted someone who translated their tools (standardised tests/measurements of behaviour) and their findings into meaningful information in the context of care proceedings. Second, like the criteria engaged in appointing psychiatrists, guardians also wanted psychologists who are known and experienced in the legal arena:

- 87 per cent said they wanted a psychologist who explains the significance of results for the particular child;

- 72 per cent wanted someone who is an experienced expert witness;

- 64 per cent wanted someone they have used before and trust;

- 63 per cent wanted someone who explains the significance of standardised tests in accessible language;

- 62 per cent wanted someone who, if necessary, would do a series of observations; and

Determining factors	%
Someone who explains the significance of results for the particular child	87
Someone who is an experienced expert witness, good in court	72
Someone I have used and trust	64
Someone who explains results of standardised tests in accessible language	63
Someone who is willing to do a series of observations	62
Someone willing/able to undertake further therapeutic work	55
Someone who is locally based	37
Someone who includes research findings in their reports	32

Table 3.3

Important factors determining choice of a psychologist to undertake an assessment of a child

Note: N = 326

- over half (55 per cent) indicated that the fact that someone was willing/ able to undertake further therapeutic work would also be an important criterion in determining choice of a psychologist.

d) Shortages of experts

In the light of growing concerns expressed by both guardians and experts about the mounting difficulties of meeting increases in demands for expert assessments and reports for court proceedings, we asked guardians whether they had experienced actually failing to find a child and adolescent psychiatrist or a psychologist to undertake an assessment for them.

Table 3.4 demonstrates that despite concerns by most professionals in this field, a complete failure to locate an expert is a relatively rare but not unknown experience: 15 per cent of the sample had tried and failed to find a child and adolescent psychiatrist to undertake an assessment on at least one occasion and nine per cent had tried and failed to find a psychologist to undertake an assessment of a child on at least one occasion.

Appointing experts	%
Tried and failed to find an adult psychiatrist	8
Tried and failed to find a child and adolescent psychiatrist	15
Tried and failed to find a psychologist to undertake an assessment of a child	9
Tried and failed to find a psychologist to undertake an assessment of an adult	7

Table 3.4

Do guardians have any experience of trying and failing to appoint experts?

Note:
N = 321 (for psychiatrists)
N = 316 (for psychologists)

In view of the anxiety expressed by some guardians in the pilot interviews about the 'nightmare of trying to find an expert', these findings may be somewhat surprising. However, two issues need to be borne in mind. First, the criteria set by guardians in selecting experts indicates that they want the 'best in the field'. Indications from this survey and from Stage III of the project are that guardians, in certain panels at least, commission "national" experts when they require expert evidence. Hence, using locally based people was not high on their criteria for appointment. Second, despite the fact that this was not an open-ended question in the survey, many guardians also commented that, although they may not have actually failed to make an appointment, they may not get their first choice or they may have to wait longer than they would wish for their first choice.

From the survey data we do not know how often guardians compromised on their first choice or indeed whether the outcome of that decision in those cases proved any more or less problematic than they had envisaged.* Moreover, we do not know the maximum period guardians are willing or able to wait to obtain the experts of their choice.

Although both the court-based study and this survey (see Table 4.9) identify child and adolescent psychiatrists as the major providers of expert evidence in care proceedings, we asked guardians if they had experienced difficulties in obtaining assessments and reports from any other specialists/disciplines: 12 per cent said they had.

We also asked whether they had experienced any difficulties in commissioning experts to provide second opinions; almost all (92 per cent) said they had not experienced any difficulties. Where difficulties had

* The project takes this issue forward in a number of ways. First, in Section II of this survey we asked for further information on experts who were being used by a guardian for the first time (see page 35). Second, in Stage II of the project (interviews with guardians from three panels) we seek qualitative information on the choice of expert and the influence of time factors; in Stage III we pursue aspects of this issue (e.g. the existence of clinical waiting lists) with a sample of experts.

occurred, guardians thought it was due to two rather different factors: an unwillingness on the part of experts to challenge colleagues or impinge on another colleague's views, or the effect of a general shortage of good people in the field.

e) Reluctant experts: the current and the potential pool

Not all specialists in the field of child and adolescent mental health and child development are able or willing to engage in the legal arena and undertake assessments, provide reports and, if necessary, appear in court to be cross-examined. The reasons for this vary from the personal views of experts about the limited value of such work and a dislike of the "adversarial" nature of proceedings, to a range of issues surrounding the expert's institutional base and particular contractual agreements with employing bodies.

The adversarial nature of family proceedings attracted much criticism prior to the introduction of the Children Act 1989. In the light of new policy objectives in this field, and specifically attempts to promote a shift towards inquisitorial proceedings*, we asked guardians in an open-ended question whether some experts nevertheless remained unwilling to do assessments and reports for courts and the reasons for that reluctance.

The responses suggest that, for some experts at least, perceptions and perhaps experiences of court work have not changed substantially since the criticisms of legal process prior to the Act. Guardians said experts expressed reluctance or were unwilling take instructions due to:

- a lack of time and work overload and a reluctance, therefore, to waste time in court;

- a conflict of interests between therapeutic work and court work;

- objections to being "grilled in court" and/or an unwillingness to expose their work to criticism;

- a lack of experience in child protection issues coupled with an anxiety provoked by the idea of giving oral evidence and being cross-examined; and

- little interest on a professional basis in this category of work. For example, they questioned the validity of assessments for courts, they saw it as "unreal" and could often only state the obvious.

f) Help in locating appropriate experts

In the wake of concern over the difficulties of locating experts both able and willing to work in the legal arena, various professional and commercial bodies have attempted to provide assistance or improve existing services to people seeking to appoint experts in legal proceedings. The Law Society has improved and updated the *Directory of Expert Witnesses* (1996), The Academy of Experts provides a similar service.† The Official Solicitor's Office is also said to provide some assistance.

This type of facility is not, however, without its problems or its critics (e.g. guardians and some experts have expressed concerns about the selection criteria for inclusion in such registers and the high reliance in some lists on experts who are retired). In pilot work with guardians we did not find a high use or reliance on these resources/directories as a source for identifying appropriate experts.

* DoH (1991a) *The Children Act 1989, Guidance and Regulations, Vol 1,* p 3.

† It should be noted, however, that such lists have no official standing, most referrals are self referral and by word of mouth. In addition, there are ethical considerations which prevent such bodies as the Royal College of Psychiatrists from providing lists of experts.

Although the "trickle down" effect* operated in some panels, guardians also expressed anxieties about one consequence of this approach: it can mean that the experts they use become overloaded and are unable to take further work from them. We therefore asked respondents whether the panels for which they worked provided any assistance in locating appropriate experts. While many guardians (58 per cent) said panels did offer some assistance (e.g. holding lists of local experts), a substantial proportion (42 per cent) said their panels did not.[†]

Summary
Assessments of "local" child and adolescent mental health services

- **Do local services meet the needs of guardians?**
  Relatively few local child and adolescent mental health services currently meet the needs of guardians and thereby locally based children and families involved in public law proceedings.

  Major areas of concern to guardians were delays in obtaining reports, lack of thoroughness in reports received, and a lack of resources within services to undertake further therapeutic work if necessary.

- **Improvements required to local services**
  Improvements required are resource and training based – guardians need more locally based services, increased resources within services, and more staff who are better trained and more experienced.

  In some areas a wider basis of expertise was needed in the form of multi-disciplinary teams within local services.

Criteria for appointing an expert

- **Appointing a child and adolescent psychiatrist**
  A particular understanding of, and sympathy with, the needs of children and families involved in legal proceedings.

  Previous experience and skills as an expert witness dominate the criteria for appointing child and adolescent psychiatrists: the experienced expert witness, good in the witness box and able to withstand cross-examination is sought after.

- **Appointing a psychologist**
  Experience in the legal arena is important.

  Additionally, psychologists who explain their findings in accessible language are needed. The presentation of standardised tests applied followed by a list of scores presented as isolated data in reports for courts is not helpful to other professionals in the legal process. Equally, explaining the significance of the results for the particular child is important.

  Guardians also wanted to appoint psychologists who, if necessary, are willing to undertake a series of observations.

The impact of shortages

- **Failure to appoint**
  Very few guardians had actually experienced a failure to appoint a psychiatrist or a psychologist – but that may mean delays in getting a first choice; few (12 per cent) had experienced difficulties in obtaining

* Whereby new guardians obtain the names of "tried and trusted" experts from more experienced colleagues.

† This represents the majority (58 per cent) of panels represented in the survey.

expertise in areas other than psychology and psychiatry.

- **The potential pool of experts**
  According to the experiences of guardians, decisions by experts *not* to undertake this type of work were based on three main considerations:

  * they were, in part, resource led (services in some areas at least are already over-stretched in meeting clinical demands);

  * a dislike of the adversarial approach; and

  * a lack of conviction about the validity of this category of work.

Finding appropriate experts

- **Using commercial registers, assistance offered by panels**
  Finding an appropriate expert can be difficult especially for new guardians. Experts on commercial lists are not necessarily an option for guardians – their selection criteria indicates they want someone whose judgement they know and trust – the "unknown quantity" may be appointed by parents but not by guardians.

  Some panels have began to offer assistance by producing lists of experts based on personal recommendations of guardians but this can lead to an overload for those specialists who are perceived as "good" expert witnesses and thus are included on panel lists.

Cases containing expert evidence

Introduction

This section of the survey aimed to address a number of substantive issues within current practices with regard to the use of experts. We asked guardians to provide information on their two most recently completed cases which involved experts. We then asked them to address a range of questions about:

- the applications, orders and outcomes of cases;

- the types of expert reports filed;

- the consultation practices of both local authorities and guardians;

- the role of the court in single party instructions;

- the impact of using experts on delay in certain cases; and

- why guardians use experts in certain cases and their experiences of using new people.

For those cases where more than one party had instructed experts and filed reports, we asked:

- how often in practice were the same issues/concerns addressed by more than one expert;

- what the implications were of multiple assessments for the child or children involved;

- why a second expert was instructed;

- how the reports compared – in terms of the assessments and recommendations and with the original order requested in the case.

We begin by providing an analysis of the cases in the survey. We then examine practices in those cases in which one party only filed expert reports. First, we examine cases where *only the local authority* provided expert reports. Second, we look at those cases in which *only the guardian* provided expert reports. Finally, we look at those cases where *more than one party* filed expert evidence; these are potentially the more complex cases.*

The sample cases – a profile

a)   *The children: age, sex, ethnicity and number of children in proceedings*

In total, we obtained data on 557 cases involving just under 1,000 (963) children and young people. The sample consisted of equal proportions of female and male children. As Table 4.1 demonstrates, 63 per cent of the sample children were six years of age or under and the proportions of female/male children in this age band are very similar. The majority of the children in the sample were white European (84 per cent – Table 4.2).

* A breakdown of cases is illustrated in Figure 4.1 on page 23.

	Boys %	Girls %	Total %
0–12 months	13	11	12
1–3 years	27	28	28
4–6 years	24	23	23
7–9 years	17	16	17
10–12 years	12	11	12
13+ years	7	11	9
TOTAL	50	50	100

Table 4.1

Age bands of children in 557 cases

Note: N = 963
(age and/or gender missing data 16)

	Ethnic group of children in sample %	Ethnic group of children aged 0–5 in England and Wales* %
White European	84	91
Black	6	2
South Asian	2	5
Other	0	1
Mixed parentage	8	1
TOTAL	100	100

Table 4.2

Ethnic identity of children in sample

Note: *1991 Census; Phoenix & Owen 1996
N = 946 (missing data 17)

* In Table 4.2, comparisons have been made between data from this survey and the 1991 Census data (OPCS/GRO(S) 1994). Some caution is necessary in interpreting this comparison because of the different ways in which data on ethnicity were collected. The Census data is based upon how people described the ethnicity of their children in responses to a given set of options. In this study guardians were asked to describe the ethnicity of the children in the sample cases. These descriptions were then coded according to the Census categories. The comparisons for children of mixed parentage were based on Phoenix and Owen (1996) who used specially commissioned Census tables. There is a suggestion (eg. Barn 1993:30) that many if not most of the children in the category "mixed parentage" are, in practice, black children of mixed parentage. Further analysis of the survey data will address this issue.

† Cases involving three children accounted for 10 per cent of all cases. Cases involving four or five (or more) children each accounted for 4 per cent of all cases.

However, black children and children of mixed parentage are over-represented in the sample compared with their presence in the general population.*

Cases which involved a single child accounted for 57 per cent of all cases and in over 80 per cent of cases, the maximum number of children involved in the proceedings was two. Thus cases involving three or more children were relatively rare.†

b) The applications, the courts and the outcomes

As Table 4.3 illustrates, the majority of cases involving experts were finalised in the higher courts. For those cases in the sample which began in the family proceedings courts (88 per cent of the total sample of cases), just over a third of cases (35 per cent) were completed in that court, but most cases (53 per cent) were transferred, 42 per cent being completed in a care centre and a further 11 per cent being completed in the High Court.

	Court of Application†		
Final Order Court*	FPC %	CC %	HC %
Family Proceedings Court (FPC)	35	n/a	n/a
Care Centre (CC)	42	7	n/a
High Court (HC)	11	1	3
TOTAL	88	8	3

Table 4.3

Courts

Note: N = 557
† Court in which the initial application was made
* Court which made the Final Order

Transferred cases	% *
Reasons for transfer:	
Complicated/conflicting evidence	82
Number of parties	26
Novel/difficult point of law	6
Question of public interest	3
Other reason	18

Table 4.4

Transferred cases

Note: * Percentages exceed 100 because reasons for transfer are not mutually exclusive.
N = 301 (based on 301 transferred cases from the total sample of 557 cases)

Not surprisingly, the major reason for transfer in these cases was complicated/conflicting expert evidence – this was one of the grounds for transfer to a higher court in well over two-thirds of cases (82 per cent of cases, see Table 4.4). Given the increased rights now extended to family members to become parties to proceedings following the Children Act 1989, it is perhaps surprising that the number of parties in a case (as one of a number of reasons for transfer) applied to only 26 per cent of the sample.*

Table 4.5 demonstrates that regardless of the number of children in the case, most *applications* in the sample were for a single order (i.e. applications were the same for all children in the case): 92 per cent of applications were of this type. Moreover, the majority of those applications were for care orders – 79 per cent of all single order applications were for care orders.

Applications made	%
Single applications made:	
Care order only	79
Supervision order only	5
Discharge care order only	2
Contact with child in care	2
Refusal of contact	2
Section 8 order*	2
Applications for two or more orders	8
TOTAL	100

Table 4.5

Applications – breakdown

Note: * From the survey data we cannot always determine precisely how cases became "specified proceedings" (and hence the appointment of a guardian). The two most obvious reasons are: 1) that the case began as a private law dispute in which the local authority made a subsequent application, and 2) an application for a section 8 order was made in respect of a child already in care.
N = 555 (missing data 2)

With regard to final orders, single orders accounted for 78 per cent of the total orders made: 48 per cent of these were for care orders. Thus, in the overall sample, 79 per cent of applications were for care orders and, in 48 per cent of cases, care orders were made (see Table 4.6). This accounted for 266 *cases* and 578 *children*. In other words, care orders were made in just under half of all *cases* in the sample, and this accounted for over half of all *children* in the sample.

However, not all children who are subject to a care order will necessarily be removed from the care of their parents. We therefore also asked guardians to provide information on the proposed care plan for those children who were subject to a care order. Although for most *cases* a single type of application and a single type of final order were the most likely (see Tables 4.5 and 4.6) regardless of the number of children in the proceedings, nevertheless the care plans proposed by local authorities for children who are subject to care orders can of course vary. Each child within a case should have an individual care plan even though in practice the care plan for all the relevant children in a case may well be the same.

* There were only nine cases in which the number of parties was the only reason for transfer.

Final orders made	%
Single orders made:	
Care order only	48
Supervision order only	11
Discharge care order	0.4
Discharge supervision order	0.2
Contact with child in care	2
Refusal of contact	2
Section 8 order	5
Other	9
Two or more orders made	22
TOTAL	**100**

Table 4.6

Final orders – breakdown

N = 557
(missing data 6)

For those 578 children subject to care orders, in most cases the local authority proposed a single care plan* and, for the majority (63 per cent), the plan was for permanent removal from parents:

- for 44 per cent, the care plan was to find a permanent substitute family;

- for a further 17 per cent the plan was for them to remain in permanent substitute care; and

- 2 per cent were to be placed in a children's home.

Only 18 per cent of this sub-sample were to be placed with parents under a care order and, in the case of a further 10 per cent, it was proposed to place children with members of their extended family (see Table 4.7).

Care plans made	%
Child to remain in permanent substitute family	17
Plans to find a permanent substitute family	44
Children placed in children's home	2
Children to be placed with parents	18
Children to be placed with extended family	10
Other	9
TOTAL	**100**

Table 4.7

Care plan for the children for whom a care order was made

Note: N = 578 (children who were subject to a care order)

* Two or more plans accoundted for 13 per cent of cases (47 cases, 21 children).

† It is not possible from the survey data to assess the degree of joint instructions in particular cases (or, for that matter, whether there is a common understanding/definition of what constitutes a "joint instruction"). With regard to the degree to which expert evidence in the sample cases was "joint", for example, this varied from a situation in which all the expert evidence in a case was jointly commissioned to situations in which one of a number of reports filed was based on joint instructions.

c) Which parties or combinations of parties appointed experts in the sample cases?

We asked guardians to identify which party or combination of parties had filed expert evidence in each of the cases for which they provided information. As Table 4.8 demonstrates, cases in which expert evidence was filed by more than one party (multiple parties filing) accounted for 46 per cent – or nearly half the total sample of cases. Cases in which *only one party* filed any expert evidence accounted for 48 per cent of cases. Cases where the guardian indicated there was *any* element of joint instructions to an expert accounted for just 6 per cent of the sample† (see Figure 4.1).

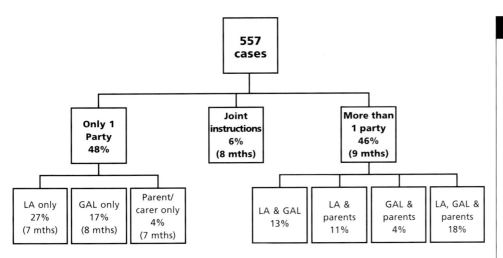

Figure 4.1

Parties which filed expert reports/ duration of cases

Party/parties filing reports	%
Cases in which only the local authority filed expert reports	27
Cases in which only the guardian filed expert reports	17
Cases in which only the parents/carers filed expert reports	4
Cases where more than one party filed expert reports	46
Cases which involved expert reports where there was an element of joint instruction	6

Table 4.8

Party or parties which filed expert reports in the cases

Note: N = 557

For the group of cases in which *one party only* filed expert reports, those in which the local authority was the only party to have filed expert reports accounted for 27 per cent of the sub-group; those in which the guardian was the only party to have filed expert reports accounted for 17 per cent of the sub-group and those in which only parents filed expert reports accounted for 5 per cent of the sub-group (see Figure 4.1).

In the light of recent prominence given to the joint instructions of experts, in addition to asking guardians to supply information on their two most recently completed cases involving experts, we also asked whether they had been involved in *any* joint instructions to an expert during the calendar year 1994. Although just over half the sample had some experience (53 per cent) nearly as many (47 per cent) did not. And, for those who had any experience of joint instructions, the degree of experience was not large – most experience was limited to one or two cases:

- 38 per cent had been involved in one case in which joint instructions had been issued to an expert

- 22 per cent had experience of two such cases

- 18 per cent had experience of three such cases.*

We also asked whether a joint instruction was in effect limited to a joint letter of instruction to an expert, or whether there was also joint funding of the costs. For most (60 per cent) it appears that a joint instruction was restricted to a joint letter of instruction – very few guardians expressed any knowledge of obtaining joint funding of an expert assessment and report.†

* 8 per cent (14 guardians) had experience of four cases; 5 per cent (9 guardians) had experience of five cases.

† Some caution may be necessary with this finding since it may be the case that guardians would not necessarily know how the costs had been allocated – particularly perhaps those guardians employed by social service departments – 16 per cent of the total sample of guardians (see Brophy, Wale & Bates, 1997).

We also asked those with experience of joint instructions whether there had been any major problems with that exercise: most (70 per cent – 96 guardians) said no. However, a substantial proportion (30 per cent – 41 guardians) said they had experienced major problems. Further research is necessary in this field but, for those who indicated having experienced problems, a preliminary analysis* suggested the following areas had proved difficult:

- difficulties in getting parties to share instructions

- problems encountered where the situation or circumstances changed and, as a consequence, instructions changed during a case

- procedures where there is a disagreement/dislike of the resulting report.

d) The dominant types of specialists commissioned

Table 4.9 illustrates two major findings from the analysis of case profiles. First, overall, psychiatrists are the major providers of expert evidence in care and related proceedings. Second, parties relied on different categories of expert evidence. Reports which included an assessment of the child(ren) formed the main category of expert evidence filed by local authorities and by guardians, while assessments of adults only provided the majority of parents' evidence:

* Based on a random sample of 55 responses to an open-ended question.

	All cases %	Local authority %		Guardian %		Parents %		Joint instruc. %
N =	(557)	(147)	(236)	(94)	(197)	(26)	(186)	(32)
Paediatric report	35	35	46	6	16	4	13	31
Paediatric radiologist's report	10	7	14	3	9	0	6	0
Other medical report	12	7	12	2	8	4	8	12
Psychiatric report on child and family	41	27	30	33	44	12	15	66
Psychiatric report on child only	11	12	7	12	7	0	4	6
Multidisciplinary report on parent(s) and child/children	15	12	11	1	4	0	14	25
Psychiatric report on parent(s)/carer(s)	32	20	20	16	16	54	33	22
Psychological report (educational) on child/children	13	14	13	6	5	0	2	16
Psychological report (clinical) on child/children	14	16	7	14	10	0	2	6
Psychological report on parents(s)/adult carer(s)	24	18	15	9	14	23	24	16
Psychological report assessing parents(s) and child/children	12	8	10	14	7	0	4	12
Report of parenting skills assessment	23	26	30	5	4	4	2	25
Psychotherapist's report on child or parent	4	3	4	1	3	0	1	3
Other expert/specialist reports	18	15	15	7	8	15	8	19

Table 4.9

Types of expert evidence which were filed by parties in the cases

Note: With regard to the parties filing, the first column denotes reports filed in those cases where that party was the only one to file expert reports in cases; the second shaded column denotes reports filed by that party in multiparty cases, that is, where they were one of a number of parties to file expert reports

- **psychiatric reports on children and families** were filed in 41 per cent of all cases. In "multiparty" cases, such reports formed:

  30 per cent of all reports filed by local authorities
  44 per cent of all reports filed by guardians
  but 15 per cent of all reports filed by parents.

- **psychiatric reports on parent(s)/carer(s)** were filed in 32 per cent of all cases. In "multiparty" cases, such reports formed:

  20 per cent of reports filed by local authorities
  16 per cent of reports filed by guardians
  33 per cent of reports filed by parents.

However, in cases where the parents were the only party filing evidence, such reports accounted for 54 per cent of all reports filed.

- **psychological reports on parent(s)/carer(s)** were filed in almost a quarter (24 per cent) of all cases. In "multiparty" cases, such reports formed:

  15 per cent of reports filed by local authorities
  14 per cent of reports filed by guardians
  24 per cent of reports filed by parents.

- **reports based on parenting skills assessments** were filed in 23 per cent of all cases. In "multiparty" cases, such reports formed:

  30 per cent of the reports filed by local authorities
  4 per cent of reports filed by guardians
  2 per cent of reports filed by parents.

- **paediatric reports** were filed in 35 per cent of all cases. In "multiparty" cases, such reports formed:

  46 per cent of reports filed by local authorities
  16 per cent of reports filed by guardians
  13 per cent of reports filed by parents.

e)   *The duration of cases*

Guardians were asked how long cases took to complete. As Table 4.10 illustrates duration ranged from under one month to three years and ten months. Fifty per cent of cases were completed in just under eight months, and the mean duration of cases was 8.3 months.

	Number	%
0–2 months	8	1
3–5 months	125	23
6–8 months	177	33
9–11 months	142	26
12–23 months	80	15
24 months and above	8	1
TOTAL	540	99*

Table 4.10

Duration of cases

Note: * Total sums to 99% due to rounding
N = 540
(missing data 17)
Mean duration = 8.32 months
Median duration = 8 months
Low = under one month
High = 46 months

In addition to the types of expert evidence filed in cases, data were also collected on a number of factors which might be expected to affect the length of a case. Four variables were constructed from the profile data we outlined above. These included the type and number of applications, the court in which a case started and whether it was transferred to a higher court, the party filing expert reports and the number of parties filing such reports, and whether there was any element of joint instructions in a case. The full statistical analyses undertaken with these variables are outlined in the Appendix. The important variables associated with duration of cases which involved experts were:

- *type of order requested* – those cases which included an application for a care order took an average of one month less to complete

- whether there was *more than one type of application* – single applications took an average of two and a quarter months less to complete

- whether the case was *transferred* – those cases which started in the family proceedings courts and were finalised in a care centre took an extra three months to complete; those cases which were transferred to the High Court took an extra four and a half months to complete

- whether *more than one party filed expert reports* – "multiparty" cases took an average of one and one-fifth months more than all other cases

Thus, variation in duration is associated with different factors. One important question is whether these factors are acting independently of each other with regard to their association with duration of cases. Taking cases which *started and were completed* in the family proceedings courts (or the care centre) as a baseline group of cases, further analyses showed that the transfer variable was the most important in explaining duration,* whereas types of application and instructing parties were less significant.†

There are a number of other factors which have an effect on the duration of cases which are absent from this model. For example, although we have highlighted the significance of transferred cases, within the confines set by the survey we were not able to ask more detailed questions about these cases. One important gap in the data is the intervals between the date of the decision to transfer and the first directions hearing in the higher court. A further important factor to be considered in this context is whether any assessments were being undertaken or completed during that period. Equally, we do not know from this data which court was responsible for granting the majority of leaves to instruct experts and how successful courts were in timetabling and monitoring the filing of that evidence.

Summary

The profile of cases

- **The children**
  Most children in the sample were aged six years or under and, whilst there were equal proportions of girls and boys, black children and children of mixed parentage were over-represented in the sample.

- **The courts**
  Just over half the sample cases transferred to a higher court – 53 per cent of cases in the sample. Complicated/conflicting expert evidence was the major reason for transfer.

* See Appendix – multiple regression analyses undertaken.

† See Table 7.2 and Appendix.

- **Applications and orders**
  Almost all original applications were for single orders (i.e. one category of order for all the children in the case) – this accounted for 92 per cent of the sample cases.

  Within single order applications, applications for care orders were the largest group accounting for 79 per cent of all such applications; 48 per cent of applications for care orders were successful – this involved 578 children, over half the sample.

  Where care orders were made, the local authority proposed a single care plan for most of the children and, for the *majority* of those children (63 per cent of those subject to a care order), the plan was to place them in a *permanent substitute household*.

- **Which parties filed expert evidence?**
  The largest category of cases in the sample were those in which expert evidence was filed by *one party only (48 per cent)*. However, the differences are not large – cases in which *more than one party* filed some expert evidence accounted for 46 per cent of cases. Cases which contained *any* element of "joint instruction" accounted for only 6 per cent of the total sample.

- **The dominant disciplines commissioned**
  With regard to the particular *disciplines* commissioned by parties:

  Child and family psychiatric reports were the largest single group (appearing in 41 per cent of all cases). Such reports were the major form of evidence filed by guardians and the second largest single category of evidence filed by local authorities.

  Adult psychiatric reports formed the majority of reports filed by parents – indeed, reports based on assessments of adults (both psychiatric and psychological) formed the major source of parents' expert evidence in the sample cases.

- **Duration of cases**
  The court where a case started and whether it was subsequently transferred was the main explanation for duration of cases.

  Cases containing applications for care orders were associated with a small decrease in duration which was independent of the start court or transfer status.

  Cases where more than one party filed expert reports were associated with a small increase in duration which was independent of the start court or transfer status, but not independent of whether the case contained an application for a care order.

Cases in which only the local authority filed expert evidence

Introduction

In this section we begin with those cases in which only one party filed any expert evidence. We start by examining those cases in which the local authority was the only party to file expert reports and where reports were based on sole instructions to experts. Table 4.9 demonstrates that the local authority was responsible for 27 per cent of such cases (147 cases) and the mean duration for this group of cases was 6.87 months (see Table 4.24).

Guardians in this sub-group of cases were asked a range of questions about the practices of local authorities and courts during the case. We also asked about the impact of expert assessments on any delay experienced in cases and whether (if expert assessments did result in delay) such delay was considered by the guardian to be prejudicial to the interests of children or parents.

a)   Types of expert evidence filed by local authorities

Where the local authority was the only party to file any expert evidence as Table 4.9 identifies, the largest single category of expert evidence filed was paediatric evidence. Paediatric radiologists' reports in fact accounted for a very small proportion (7 per cent) of local authority evidence in these cases.* Psychiatric reports which focused on both children and parents were filed in 27 per cent of cases and expert reports based on an assessment of parenting skills were filed in just over a quarter of these cases. Thus, where the local authority was the only party to file any expert evidence, paediatric, psychiatric and parenting skills assessments were the dominant forms of expert evidence sought and filed.[†]

b)   Were experts needed? – the views of the guardian

We asked guardians whether they agreed with the local authority decision to seek expert evidence – did they agree that there was in fact a need for *expert* evidence in a particular case? Almost all the guardians in these cases (95 per cent) agreed with the local authority's decision to seek expertise beyond those of the social workers in the case.

c)   Levels of consultation undertaken by local authorities about the use of experts

Local authorities are expected to work in partnership with parents and to take account of their wishes.[**] However, it is sometimes suggested that the instigation of legal proceedings is indicative that all attempts at partnership have broken down. Nevertheless, it is arguably the case that such proceedings should not necessarily suspend a local authority's responsibility to attempt to consult with parents – since the same kind of approach should be taken (i.e. working with and where possible consulting parents) *after* compulsory measures have resulted in a care order.[††] Consulting with parents about decisions about the use of experts during proceedings may be one important component in understanding the perspective taken by parents during proceedings, and may have implications for later attempts at working in partnership with them.

There are, however, some circumstances where it is not always possible to consult other parties about the need for and the choice of a particular expert. For example, an expert's involvement may be the result of an emergency or follow from clinical work already undertaken with a family which predated proceedings, or an expert's involvement in current proceedings can be a consequence of involvement in previous proceedings. Equally, where there are suspicions of Munchausen's syndrome by proxy or allegations of sexual abuse, the use of experts and the degree of consultation and involvement with parents in choosing experts is often not possible or is particularly complex.

However, where experts were instructed *within* proceedings and where other parties were not a party to those instructions (e.g. where experts are not jointly instructed and/or where experts may not have been an agreed choice), we attempted to ascertain how much consultation was routinely undertaken by local authorities with both the guardian and the parents in the case.

* Although this figure increases to 14 per cent where the local authority is one of a number of parties filing such reports ("multiparty" cases) it remains relatively low.

† And that pattern is repeated in cases where the local authority is one of a number of parties filing expert reports – see Table 4.9.

** *Working Together under the Children Act*, DoH (1991); *The Challenge of Partnership* DoH (1995)

†† DoH (1991c) *The Children Act 1989, Guidance and Regulations, Vol 3 Family Placements*, p.4, para 2.12 (a), (b) and (c).

Local authority consultations with guardians	Yes %	No %	Total %
Did the local authority consult the guardian:			
• About the need for expert assessments	83	17	100
• Over the choice of a specific expert to undertake the assessment	61	39	100

4 Expert evidence

Table 4.11

In cases of single party instructions to experts by local authorities, how much consultation did they routinely undertake with guardians?

Note: N = 156

Tables 4.11 and 4.12 demonstrate that in most cases the local authorities had consulted with the guardian more often than with parents over both the need for an expert and the choice of a particular expert to undertake an assessment/examination of a child:

• 83 per cent of guardians were consulted over the question of whether an expert was needed

• 61 per cent were also consulted over the choice of a particular expert to provide the assessment.

This relatively high degree of consultation with guardians is not perhaps surprising since guardians are under a duty to advise the court on these issues. Thus, good and pragmatic practice would indicate that local authorities should ascertain the guardian's views when seeking to appoint experts.

Addressing the question of consultation with parents is a more problematic exercise for several reasons. First, examining whether local authorities routinely discussed the need for and choice of experts with parents in the absence of direct access to the parents is unsatisfactory. Asking guardians as a secondary source about this issue can only provide a starting point for further work. Moreover, as indicated above, the very notion of "consultation" with parents about using experts in the context of care proceedings can in practice be a complex issue.*

As a starting point for further work in this field, we asked guardians whether local authorities had consulted with parents in these cases. Table 4.12 demonstrates that in those cases where expert evidence was commissioned within proceedings:

• 65 per cent of guardians said parents had been consulted by the local authority about the need for that evidence, but a much smaller proportion (34 per cent) said parents had also been consulted over the choice of a specific expert to undertake the examination/assessment.

* We address this issue in more depth elsewhere (Brophy & Bates, 1998) *The Position of Parents Using Experts in Care Proceedings*

Local authority consultations with parents	Yes %	No %	Don't know %	Not possible %	Total %
Did the local authority consult with parents:					
• About the need for expert assessment*	65	21	11	3	100
• Over the choice of expert to undertake the assessment**	34	44	17	5	100

Table 4.12

In cases of single party instructions to experts by local authorities, how much consultation did they routinely undertake with parents?

Note: * missing data 1
** missing data 3
N = 148

Only a small number of guardians did not know whether local authorities had consulted with parents, 11 per cent said they did not know whether parents had been consulted over the need for experts, but 17 per cent said they did not know if parents had been consulted over choice. Less than 5 per cent of guardians said it had not been possible to consult with parents.

d)   Court control over proceedings: opportunities to explore the possibility of a joint instruction

As this sub-sample of cases was based on sole instructions to an expert by one party (the local authority), it enabled us to ask guardians whether the court had attempted to encourage the local authority to seek to instruct the expert(s) jointly with any other party.

In most cases it appears courts had not taken the initiative: 84 per cent of guardians said courts had not attempted to encourage the local authority to seek the involvement of other parties in instructions to experts. Only 16 per cent said the court had encouraged the local authority to try this route, although inclusion of the case in this sub-group indicates that whilst encouraged to do so by the court, the local authority (for whatever reason) was either unsuccessful in negotiating joint instructions with any other party or chose not to pursue that route.

e)   Expert assessments and delay

The Children Act 1989 states as a general principle that any delay is likely to prejudice the welfare of the child.* Nevertheless, research continues to identify the fact that cases take considerably longer than the 12 week "bench mark" much in discussion in the early days of the Act (CAAC 1991/2; 1994/5). Although we lacked systematic evidence, difficulties in appointing experts has lent support to the view that, in some geographical locations at least, clinic waiting lists meant that appointing experts was perhaps contributing to the overall length of cases.

Analysing the impact of instructing experts on the duration of cases is a complex exercise. There are a range of interrelated and compounding issues. For example, the quality of work already undertaken by local authorities (e.g. the "orange" book assessment)† may have an impact on the degree of subsequent "family assessment" work undertaken by experts. The existence of prior expert reports in a case, the stage in proceedings at which a case is referred, the range of questions to be addressed by experts, their own waiting lists, the number of clinical appointments necessary for the assessment, the number of experts ultimately involved in the case and the time taken to file reports – these are all relevant and compounding factors.

Equally, where the case is contested, the point at which it ceases to be contested and the availability of court dates have an impact on length of cases. It is also in a child's interests that all the possible alternative options which might exist prior to making a court order be considered. Therefore, some delay in cases can be seen as "purposeful"; that is, where it serves some constructive purpose in trying to find a resolution to the issues. One example might be "delaying" a case so that parents can undertake a residential placement for an assessment of parenting skills.

Within the confines set by quantitative methods, we sought to isolate a sample of cases where we could control for at least some of the above compounding issues, for example, cases where only one party filed expert reports and where guardians agreed that expert evidence was necessary, and to try to distinguish the different types of delay which might have occurred.

* Children Act 1989, s. 1(2).

† DoH (1988), *Protecting Children: A Guide for Social Workers undertaking a Comprehensive Assessment.*

Are experts causing delay?	%
Yes	22
No	59
Case was adjoined for assessment over time to take place	19
TOTAL	100

Table 4.13

Did expert assessments/ examinations *in themselves* result in delay?

Note: N = 148
(missing data 1)

In this sub-sample of 147 cases, therefore, we asked guardians whether expert assessments or examinations *per se* resulted in delay in the case, the reasons for any delay incurred, and whether the guardian considered delay was prejudicial to children and/or parents.

i) Have experts caused delay in these cases?
As Table 4.13 demonstrates, most guardians (59 per cent) said expert assessments had not *per se* resulted in delay. Nevertheless, as Table 4.24 demonstrates, the mean duration for this group of cases was almost seven months. Thus, whatever other factors impeded the speedy completion of these applications, delay was due to expert assessments/examinations in less than a quarter of cases.

ii) Where expert evidence had resulted in some delay, what were the reasons?
For those 22 per cent of cases where expert assessments had caused delay, we asked guardians to identify the reasons. As Table 4.14 shows, the inability of experts to complete assessments in the specified period or to file the report on time was identified in 38 per cent and 11 per cent of cases respectively. Notably, the failure of parents to keep appointments with experts (often suggested as a major reason for delay in filing expert reports) was identified by less than a quarter of guardians (22 per cent) as a reason for delay in this sub-group of cases.

Reasons for delay	%
Local authority experienced problems in finding an expert	14
Assessment took case over presumptive framework	22
Appointments were not kept by parents	22
Experts did not complete assessment in required period	38
Assessment/examination was completed in time but report was late	11
Other reasons	24

Table 4.14

Reasons for delay resulting from expert examination/assessment

Note: N = 33

iii) Was delay prejudicial to the interests of children or parents?
We also asked guardians if they considered the delay experienced in these cases was prejudicial to the interests/welfare of the child and/or the parent(s). Guardians indicated for most children (55 per cent) and for most parents (64 per cent) it was not.* However, for 36 per cent of children and 12 per cent of parents the delay incurred by expert assessments was considered by the guardian to be prejudicial to their interests.

iv) "Purposeful" delay
As Table 4.13 demonstrates 19 per cent of guardians in this sub-sample of cases indicated that the case was adjourned in order for an "assessment over time" to take place. We also asked guardians in this sub-group of cases whether they considered the resulting "purposeful" delay was, nevertheless,

* Again it should be noted that this represents the view of the guardians and it may not correspond with the views of relevant parents.

prejudicial to the intersts of child(ren) and/or parent(s). Most guardians said it was not prejudicial to the child(ren) or the parent(s) (68 per cent and 64 per cent respectively).

Summary

Local authorities' use of experts: cases where they were the only party to instruct experts and where reports were based on sole instructions

- **The disciplines appointed**
  The main types of expertise commissioned by local authorities where they were the only party instructing experts and filing reports were psychiatric, paediatric and parenting skills assessments.

- **Appropriate use of experts**
  Most decisions by local authorities to seek expert evidence were supported by the guardian appointed to the case. There was no evidence that local authorities were seeking experts in circumstances which guardians considered to be inappropriate.

  However, from the survey data it is not possible to ascertain why the guardian supported the local authority's decision. For example, it could have been because the guardian agreed the case demanded expertise beyond those of the social worker. Alternatively, it may have been because the guardian was aware of limitations within a particular local authority (eg. inexperienced social workers and/or lack of resources).

- **"Partnership" within legal proceedings – consulting with other parties**
  Local authorities consulted with *some* parents and *most* guardians about the need for and choice of experts. However, they were much more likely to consult with guardians – about one-third of parents were not consulted about the need for expert evidence and almost two-thirds of parents were not consulted about the specific choice of expert.

- **Directions hearings – an opportunity for court intervention?**
  The courts in this sub-sample did not take an active role in encouraging local authorities to engage other parties in joint instructions of experts.

- **The experts' role in delay**
  Experts were not identified by guardians as the major sources of delay in this sub-sample of cases. Where delay was experienced, for the most part, guardians did not consider it was prejudicial to the interests of the majority of children or parents.

  For those cases where some delay was experienced, the failure of experts to do assessments and reports on time was identified more frequently as a cause of delay than failures on the part of parents to keep appointments with experts.

- **Duration**
  The mean duration for those cases in which the local authority was the only party to file any expert reports was 6.87 months.

Cases in which only the guardian filed expert reports

Introduction

Cases in which only the guardian filed any expert evidence accounted for 17 per cent of cases (94 cases – see Table 4.8) and the mean duration for these cases was eight months. Guardians' use of experts is a controversial area and undergoing considerable change. In the early days following the Children Act there was some albeit unsubstantiated suggestion that perhaps guardians were resorting to experts too often or in inappropriate circumstances.*

The court-based study provided evidence that guardians were not in fact the major party instructing experts in care proceedings (Bates & Brophy, forthcoming; see also Foster & Preston Shoot, 1995). However, subsequent practice directions indicate that this position may change. For example, it has been suggested that where expert evidence is required in a case, it should normally be obtained by the guardian.[†] We therefore sought to address a range of questions in those cases in which the guardian was the only party to file expert reports.

We begin below by highlighting the types of expert evidence most commonly commissioned by guardians where they are the only party to instruct experts. Secondly, we asked whether they considered they had obtained evidence which should have been obtained by the applicant. Thirdly, we asked whether there was any attempt by the court to encourage a joint instruction in the case. Fourthly, we asked the guardian whether he or she consulted with other parties in the case about the need for, and the choice of an expert to undertake an assessment/examination.

In this section, we also asked guardians to indicate why they were the only party seeking expert evidence in the case. Finally, in addressing the issue of scarcity of experts in this field and the risks perceived in instructing specialists not previously used, we asked if, in practice, they were using any "new" people and if so, as one measure of satisfaction, whether they would instruct them a second time.

We begin by identifying the categories of experts instructed by guardians in this sub-group of cases.

a)   Types of expert evidence filed by the guardian

As Table 4.9 demonstrates, psychiatric reports on children and parents provided the major form of expert evidence commissioned by guardians** – reports of this type were filed in 33 per cent of those cases in which only the guardian filed any expert evidence.

b)   Did the guardian obtain expert evidence which should have been provided by an applicant?

The majority of guardians (66 per cent) did not consider they had obtained evidence which should have been provided by the applicant. However, just over a third (34 per cent) indicated that they had. In almost all these cases (91 per cent) the applicant was the local authority.

c)   Court control over proceedings: opportunities to explore the possibility of joint instruction?

In most of these cases (85 per cent) guardians indicated that the courts had not attempted to encourage a joint instruction of the expert or experts. Only 11 per cent reported that the court had attempted to encourage the guardians to seek a joint instruction. As with the sub-sample of cases in which the local authority was the only party instructing experts, the inclusion of cases in this section with no indication of any joint instructions suggests that for whatever reason either the guardian was not successful in obtaining a joint instruction or chose not to pursue that route.

* For example, conference discussion/ feedback: Wolkind – 1994; IRCHIN – 1994. It has also been subsequently suggested there is perhaps some reluctance on the part of guardians to appoint experts in appropriate cases, see Wall, 1995.

† Re G (Minor) (Expert Witness) [1994] 2 FLR 291 (Wall J).

** And a similar pattern emerges in those cases where the guardian is one of a number of parties filing reports (multiparty cases), see Table 4.9.

d)   Levels of consultation undertaken by guardians about the use of experts

As we discussed above, in cases where a party is intending to instruct an expert, good practice suggests that, where it is not possible or appropriate to issue joint instructions to an expert, other parties should nevertheless be consulted. Guidance on this appears to be clearer with regard to the duty of the guardian than with that of the local authority. The guardian is expected to ascertain the views of the child and the position of other parties regarding any assessments.* Therefore, in parallel with the question in the preceding section based on cases in which the local authority was the only party to instruct experts, in this sub-sample of cases we also asked about the guardian's practices of consultation.

Table 4.15 demonstrates that guardians consulted local authorities more often than parents. This applied both in relation to the need for an expert and the choice of a particular expert:

- Not surprisingly, 85 per cent of guardians indicated they had consulted the local authority, but only 67 per cent had consulted with parents about the need for an expert assessment/examination in the case.

- 59 per cent of guardians consulted local authorities about the choice of a specific expert to undertake the assessment compared with 33 per cent who consulted with parents over this issue.

Table 4.15

Consultation undertaken in cases of single party instructions to experts by the guardian.

Note: * N = 94
** N = 92

Consultations by guardians	Local authority %	Parents %	Others %	No consultation %
Consulted about the need for expert assessments*	85	67	28	7
Consulted about the choice of a specific expert to undertake the assessment**	59	33	30	21

e)   Why was the guardian the only party to seek expert evidence?

The main reason underlying the guardian's use of experts in this sample of cases was not because of disagreements with local authorities as to whether an expert was needed, or because cases were considered by the guardian to be "borderline". Rather, as Table 4.16 demonstrates, it was a result of agreement between the local authority and the guardian that expert evidence was necessary, and that the guardian should commission it. This was identified as the reason in two-thirds (67 per cent) of all cases in this sub-sample.

However, a substantial group of guardians (44 per cent) also reported that they had instructed experts to clarify their own ideas where there was a measure of doubt. A recurrent theme in discussions during the pilot interviews when considering cases in which guardians had been the only party instructing experts was, for example, 'Well, I couldn't identify it but I just knew something was not quite right'; 'I just had a gut feeling we were missing something'. "Gut feelings" were usually surrounding doubt. Perhaps this could be called "professional intuition". In addition, just over a third of the sample said they had instructed an expert because they felt the case required an assessment of a child's development.

* DoH (1991a) *The Children Act 1989, Guidance and Regulations: Vol 1, Court Orders*, p 31, para 3.49.

Reasons	%
It was agreed between the local authority and the guardian that expert evidence was necessary and that the guardian should commission it	67
It was agreed between the parent(s) and guardian that expert evidence was necessary and that the guardian should commission it	38
To clarify the guardian's own ideas where there was some measure of doubt	44
Because the guardian felt the case required an assessment of the child/children's development	34

Table 4.16

Reasons why the guardian was the only party seeking expert evidence

Note: N = 94

f) Were guardians satisfied with the work of experts they commissioned?

Most guardians were satisfied with the work of experts and this applies to both the assessments undertaken and any recommendations made – 88 per cent said they were satisfied with both assessments and any recommendations made.

g) Using new specialists

Finally, we asked guardians in this sub-sample whether they had used the particular expert before, and for those who had commissioned experts they had not previously instructed, we asked whether they would instruct that particular expert again. Most guardians (65 per cent) had in fact instructed experts they had *not* previously used – and almost all of them (93 per cent) said they would use that particular expert again.

Summary

The guardians' use of experts: cases where they were the only party to have instructed experts and where reports were based on sole instructions

- **The disciplines appointed**
  The dominant specialist instructed by guardians was a child psychiatrist; psychiatric reports on the child(ren) and family constituted the largest single category of expert reports accounting for 33 per cent of all reports filed in this sub-sample of cases.

- **"Essential evidence" in cases and the contribution of the guardian**
  Where guardians were the only party seeking expert evidence, most did not consider they had obtained evidence which should have been provided by the applicant.

  However, just over one-third (34 per cent) indicated they had obtained expert evidence which, in their view, should have been supplied by the applicant. In almost all cases, the applicant was the local authority.

- **"Partnership" within legal proceedings – consulting with other parties**
  When appointing experts, guardians consulted less with parents than with local authorities over both the need for, and choice of, a particular expert.

- **Directions hearings, an opportunity for court intervention?**
  Most courts hearing this sub-sample of cases did not take an active role in encouraging guardians to seek joint instructions.

• **Reasons for seeking expert assessments**
Where guardians were the only party seeking expert evidence, in most cases it was the result of an *agreement* – between the local authority and the guardian or the guardian and the parents – that such evidence was necessary and that the guardian should obtain it.

• **Satisfaction with the work of experts**
Most guardians are satisfied with the work undertaken by the experts they instruct.

• **Using new specialists**
Despite a stated resistance by guardians in certain panels to using specialists not previously instructed by themselves or colleagues, and the high priority given to the "known expert witness", the survey indicates that in fact guardians are using people they have not previously used.

However, it is doubtful if they are using people completely unknown – it is more likely the case that the experts used have been observed in other public law proceedings when acting under instructions from other parties or have been recommended by other guardians/panels.*

• **Duration**
The mean duration in cases in which the guardian was the only party to instruct experts was eight months.

Cases where more than one party filed expert evidence

Introduction

Finally, in this section we examine those cases in which *more than one party* filed expert reports. This group of cases constituted 46 per cent of all cases in the survey (see Table 4.18/Figure 4.1) and the mean duration for completion of these cases was nine months (see Table 4.24). Within this group, cases in which *all three parties* filed expert evidence were the largest single sub-sample representing 18 per cent of all cases (see Figure 4.1). Cases in which more than one party files expert evidence are likely to have a number of distinctive features. They clearly have the potential for competing expert opinions both within and across disciplines, they are more likely to be transferred to a higher court and, not surprisingly, they are likely to take longer to resolve.

However, it is not necessarily the case that because two experts/specialists of the same discipline are involved in a case, that they are necessarily addressing the same issues or concerns. We therefore asked guardians in this group of cases to identify whether, in practice, there were any multiple examinations and/or assessments of the same issues or concerns (e.g. two psychologists assessing "risk", two paediatric-radiologists and/or a biochemist assessing radiological evidence).

It is now accepted by professionals involved in care proceedings that from the child's perspective, multiple examinations/assessments are best avoided. Nevertheless, we asked guardians about the impact of any multiple assessments/examinations of the same issues on children, in terms of the number of face-to-face assessments in which they were involved. In addition, where parties other than the guardian commissioned a second opinion, we asked guardians to identify the reasons why this had been sought and to identify the benefits and the problems encountered. Importantly, for those cases where the guardian commissioned further expert evidence on an issue already addressed in an existing report, we also asked the reasons for that decision.

* There is for example, some evidence from Stage III of the project that panels in certain regions have shared lists of experts.

36

Assessing the contributions which experts might make in care proceedings is an extremely complex exercise. In terms of research methodologies it demands that the broad themes addressed in the survey method are complemented by deeper inferences made from qualitative examination.* One theme which can, however, be addressed at a general level is the degree to which, where parties have instructed experts to address the same issues and concerns, the resulting reports are in any way compatible. For example, does "more" in this context mean "better" evidence by, for example, ensuring the court has access to a wider knowledge base, a range of possible views and options and the benefits of different perspectives. Alternatively, does it usually mean simply more of the same, that is, a number of experts saying the same things?

We therefore asked guardians to compare some of the assessments and recommendations made by experts.†

In addition to looking at the guardians' views about the degree of diversity between reports, we also asked them to identify where experts made recommendations which differed from the order requested in the case.

Finally, we addressed the issue of parents' evidence in this category of cases; we asked what access parents' experts had to the child or children in the case and whether parents' experts prepared reports on full or partial disclosure of existing documents in the case. We begin below with the issue of conflicting expert evidence.

a)   *How often were the same issues/concerns addressed by more than one expert, what were the implications for children?*

Having identified the proportion of cases in the sample which contained a potential for overlap (Table 4.4 shows that 82 per cent of all transferred cases were transferred because of conflicting/complex expert evidence or because there was a potential for this), we asked guardians to identify those cases where they considered there was actual overlap, that is, cases where there was, in practice, more than one expert addressing the same issues or concerns.

Guardians identified that, in 65 per cent of cases in this sub-sample, reports were filed which had addressed the same issues or concerns. We then asked whether this had involved more than one *face-to-face*** examination or assessment of the child or children in the case. Just under one-third (31 per cent) said this had involved the child(ren) in more than one *face-to-face* assessment or examination.

b)   *Local authorities, parents and second reports: what were the issues?*

Where a party other than the guardian sought a second opinion on an existing report we asked guardians if they could describe (in an open-ended question) the areas or issues of disagreement generated by the first expert's report, and the reasons why a second opinion had been sought. Again, this is not an ideal method but in the absence of direct access to parents in particular, it serves as a starting point for further examination of such questions with parents themselves.

A limited analysis of the reasons given by guardians tended to focus on "disagreement" about the existing evidence without identifying the specific nature of the disagreement except in very general terms. Table 4.17 illustrates that "parental disagreement" with medical evidence (in cases of

* We take this issue further in Stages II and III of the project during interviews with guardians and mental health specialists.

† This approach is not without problems since the guardian is not an "unbiased observer" in these cases but rather a participant in the proceedings. In these data we can identify a guardian's decision to appoint a (potentially) "competing" expert but we cannot, of course, identify whether the local authority or the parents' decision to appoint an expert was to augment or dispute existing evidence.

** We employed this term to differentiate interactive assessments (i.e those in which experts have direct contact with children) from those in which experts prepared reports based on an assessment of papers only.

Reasons
Parents disagreed with local authority's medical evidence in alleged non-accidental injury
Parents disagreed with mental health evidence
Multiple disagreements between parents and the local authority
Inadequate first report (i.e. bias, limited or too narrow)

alleged non-accidental injury) and mental health evidence, or multiple disagreements between parties, are reasons for the second report. Some criticisms were made of the quality of existing reports. For example, some earlier reports were said to be biased, too narrow in scope, and/or limited in comprehensiveness.

i) The benefits/problems of second reports
We also asked guardians in an open-ended question to identify what they perceived to be the benefits and problems of obtaining that second expert's report. With regard to the benefits for parents, responses fell into two categories. First, it was seen in terms of social justice – parents have a right to instruct experts and present their case. It was also said that where the second expert report actually confirmed the views and recommendations of the earlier report, this can help parents to come to terms with difficult decisions, for example, the removal of a child, or the denial of contact with a child already in care (Table 4.18).

Second opinions
Problems
Process can prolong denial in responses of parents
Can lead to spiral of expert evidence – either conflicting or with differences of emphasis
Accessing the weight given to and value of paper reviews/assessment
Benefits
Natural justice – parents have a right to instruct their own experts and present their case in court
It can often, in confirming the view/recommendation of the first expert, help parents come to terms with a difficult decision
Adds new/different perspective
Can clarify issues

Some guardians also said that second reports had added a new/different perspective to the issues and options, and some said that the second opinion had helped to clarify issues in the case.

With regard to the problems identified with second opinions, it was stated that the process of obtaining the report had prolonged parental denial, and it had led to a spiral of expert evidence. This was not necessarily always conflicting, sometimes it had a different emphasis. Moreover, some guardians also stated that second reports in this context had raised problems for them with regard to considering how to compare reports and the weight and value to be placed on paper reviews/assessments.

ii) Comparing reports: the recommendations made by parents' experts and those contained in a previous report

We asked guardians to compare the recommendations made by parents' experts with those contained in a previous report filed by another party (i.e. a report filed by the local authority or the guardian). Table 4.19 demonstrates that, in this sample of 170 cases, a substantial proportion of

4 Expert evidence

Table 4.19

Comparing the recommendations of experts: those commissioned by a local authority/those commissioned by parents(s)

Note: N = 170 (based on those cases where more than one party filed expert evidence and where guardians indicated that the local authority and the parent(s) filed reports which addressed the same issues/concerns)

	Yes %	In part %	No %	Reports not in practice comparable %	No recom- mendations in first report %
Did the second report support any recommendations made by the first expert?	41	30	18	6	4

experts appointed by parents (41 per cent) appeared to be been in agreement with a former expert with regard to the recommendations which should be made in the specific case. A slightly higher proportion (48 per cent) identified some level of disagreement. While outright disagreement was not very high (18 per cent), partial disagreement over the appropriate recommendations to make was identified in 30 per cent of cases. In other words, in this sub-sample there was evidence of both agreement and disagreement amongst experts as to what recommendations should be made to the court.

One option for dealing with disagreements between experts is to seek the views of a further expert. This is likely to take the form of a "paper exercise" which involves asking a further expert to give an opinion based on an assessment of the existing documents and reports. We therefore also asked guardians in these cases whether there had been any further expert evidence addressing the same issues/concerns. In 38 per cent of cases (64) guardians indicated there had been a further (third) report. In 34 per cent of these, the local authority had commissioned the third report, in 26 per cent of cases it was commissioned by the guardians and in 31 per cent of cases it was commissioned by the parents.

Comparisons at this level become rather complex. We therefore decided to simply ask the guardian whether this further (third) report supported the application requested. Table 4.20 demonstrates that 42 per cent of these reports had not in fact addressed the application. However, 40 per cent did support the application, but 18 per cent did not.

	%
Report did not address the order	42
Report supported the order requested	40
Report did not support the order requested	18
TOTAL	100

Table 4.20

Did the third report support the order requested?

N = 62 (missing data 2) (based on 62 cases where a third report was filed on the same issues/concerns addressed in *two* previous reports)

c)   Guardians and second reports: what were the issues?

Guardians commissioned further expert evidence on substantially the same issues/concerns as those addressed in a previous report in 47 per cent of cases in this sub-group (79 cases). We asked guardians (in a forced choice question) to identify the reasons why they had sought further evidence. Table 4.21 illustrates that the major reasons focused on the quality and comprehensiveness of existing reports rather than changes in circumstances or because parents actually wanted a second opinion:

Reasons	%
Problems with existing report: too narrow, insufficient or inconclusive information	51
Guardian has doubts/feeling that something was being missed and therefore needed a second opinion	35
Did not include research or alternative clinical view/ perspective	28
Guardian disagreed with care plan	19
Guardian disagreed with first expert and needed own expert to say so	19
Parents wanted a second opinion	15
Case was borderline	13
Child's solicitor wanted a second opinion	12
Existing report paid insufficient attention to ethnicity/gender/class/religion/disability	12
Child wanted something quite different	7
Other reasons	46

Table 4.21

Reasons why guardian sought further assessment/examination

Note: N = 79 (based on those cases in which the guardian sought further expert evidence on issues/concerns already addressed in a previous report)

- Just over half (51 per cent) of guardians said that an existing report was too narrow and/or contained insufficient/inconclusive information.

- 35 per cent sought the opinion of a second expert in circumstances where their "professional intuition" indicated something was being missed in a case and they wanted a further expert's assessment.

- Over a quarter (28 per cent) also sought second reports because existing reports did not include the relevant research or refer to alternative clinical opinion on the issues under consideration.

d) Comparing reports commissioned by guardians with a previous report

Table 4.22 demonstrates there was also some divergence of views amongst experts commissioned in this sub-group of cases. Although the numbers are

* From the survey data we cannot identify the degree/severity of disagreement amongst experts.

	Yes %	No %	In part %	No recomenda-tions made in previous report %	Total %
Comparing recommendations:* Did the recommendations made by guardian's expert (a second opinion) confirm those made in a previous expert's report?	23	32	19	26	100
Comparing assessments:** Did guardian's expert (a second opinion) support the assessment made in a previous expert's report?	40	34	26	n/a	100
Addressing the order:*** Did the expert appointed by guardian support the order requested?	59	25	16	n/a	100

Table 4.22

Comparing the assessments/ recommendations of experts: report commissioned by guardian compared with a previous report

Note: N = 79
* missing data 10
** missing data 4
*** missing data 11
(based on cases where more than one party filed expert reports and where the guardian commissioned further expert evidence on an issue/concern already addressed in an existing report in the case)

relatively small (79 cases) about one-third of experts commissioned by guardians indicated disagreement with both the assessment and the recommendations made in a report by a previous expert. The levels of disagreement increase to 51 per cent and 60 per cent respectively if "partial" disagreements with assessments and recommendations are included.*

e) Did the expert commissioned by the guardian support the order requested?

Most experts (59 per cent) commissioned by the guardian did in fact support the *order* requested. However, 41 per cent either did not support or only partially supported the order requested.

f) Second opinions: the types of evidence filed by parents

We have reported elsewhere* that there are some significant differences in the timing and content of expert evidence filed by parents when compared with that filed by other parties in care proceedings. In particular, the court-study (Bates & Brophy, forthcoming) showed that parents were unlikely to be granted leave of the court for an expert of their choice to have direct access to children. In almost all cases, leave of the court permitting parents' experts to undertake an assessment of a child was restricted to "by way of observation only". In this survey we sought to examine whether the patterns identified in one geographical location were representative of more general trends in the compilation of expert evidence in this field of family law.

For this subgroup of cases, therefore, we asked whether the parents or other carers/potential carers had sought leave (i.e. permission) of the court for an expert examination/assessment of a child, and if so, whether that application had been successful.

	%	Was the application successful %	Assessment of child restricted to an observation only* %
No	72	n/a	n/a
Yes	28	49	18

Table 4.23

Cases where parents/potential carers filed expert reports: did parents seek leave of the court for their expert to undertake an examination/assessment of a child(ren)?

Note: N = 258 (based on those cases where more than one party filed expert reports)

Table 4.23 demonstrates that the majority of parents/potential carers (72 per cent) had not in fact sought permission of the court to instruct an expert to assess/examine their child(ren). Of those (28 per cent) who had made such an application, a third were not successful and 18 per cent obtained a restricted direction for an expert to assess the child(ren) on the basis of an observation only.

We also asked guardians whether in these cases the court had granted leave to disclose existing documents/reports in the case to experts appointed by parents – most (76 per cent) had. However, a small but not insignificant group (24 per cent) indicated that the court had not granted leave to disclose existing documents to experts appointed by parents.

Summary

Cases where more than one party filed expert evidence

- Cases in which more than one party filed expert reports constituted 46 per cent of all cases in the sample.

* Brophy & Bates (1998); Bates & Brophy (forthcoming).

- The mean duration for such cases was 9.38 months.

- Within this sample of cases, those in which *all three parties* filed expert reports were the single largest sub-group, accounting for 18 per cent of cases.

Multiple assessments by experts of the same issues/concerns

- Over half of all cases in this category (65 per cent) contained more than one report which addressed the same issues/concerns.

- Under a third of those cases (31 per cent) had involved children in more than one assessment/examination.

The recommendations of experts

Cases in which both the local authority and the parents instructed experts to address the same issues/concerns:

- Although a substantial proportion of the *recommendations* made by experts for local authorities and parents were in agreement (40 per cent), nevertheless a slightly larger proportion (48 per cent) were either not in agreement or only partially agreed.

- The benefits of second opinions for parents were identified in terms of social justice (parent have a right to appoint their expert) and, where second reports confirmed the views of a former expert, guardians thought this had a value in sometimes helping parents to "come to terms" with difficult decisions about a future order/placement of a child.

- Guardians identified the limitations of second opinions on two levels: on a practical level obtaining second opinions can prolong "parental denial" and possibly lead to a spiralling of evidence gathering, but equally such (second) reports often reflected the complexity of some of the underlying issues and this made assessments of multiple reports difficult.

Cases in which a guardian sought a second expert opinion

- Guardians were responsible for commissioning further reports on the same issues or concerns as those addressed in a previous report in 47 per cent of cases.

- In just over half of those cases (51 per cent) the guardian's reasons for the second report were related to the limited quality of an existing report.

- The level of agreement between experts appointed by guardians and experts appointed by others was not high – either with regard to the assessment or the appropriate recommendation(s) in the case:

  - 40 per cent supported a previous assessment, 23 per cent confirmed a previous recommendation

  - In over half of these cases, the experts appointed by the guardians expressed a level of disagreement with both the assessment and recommendations contained in a previous expert report (in about a third of cases it appears there was strong disagreement).

The experts instructed by parents

- Most parents did not seek leave of the court for their experts to directly assess/examine the child; where they did, few were successful in obtaining this type of assessment.

- A small number of experts instructed by parents (24 per cent) had not had access to all the documents in the case when preparing their report.

- Many expert reports filed by parents focused on the adults rather than the child in the case and many did not address the question of appropriate court orders for the relevant child(ren).

- Where experts appointed by parents had addressed the question of the appropriate court order(s) in a case, they did not always oppose the order requested. Contrary to popular belief, experts appointed by parents were not always unanimous in their support of parents.

5

Summary and discussion

Professional practices and the responses of parents in care proceedings following the Children Act 1989 have been characterised by a move towards increased use of experts. Estimates of the percentage of cases which involved experts for the calendar year 1994 all point in the same direction: all parties have increased their use of specialists since the Children Act. These estimates from a national sample support findings on the high use of experts identified in a court-based study undertaken in one geographical area.* The reasons for this apparent shift in practice are complex. The relationship between changes to law and legal procedure and the responses of both institutions and professions is clearly multifarious and geographically diverse. However, a number of factors are central to future discussions.

a)   Changes to law

First, the conditions for making a care or supervision order (the threshold criteria): the need to establish, firstly, that the child concerned is suffering, or is likely to suffer *significant harm* and secondly, that the harm or *likelihood of harm*, is attributable to the care given to the child, or *likely to be given* to him, if the order were not made, *not being what it would be reasonable to expect a parent to give him* coupled with the definitions of harm incorporated into the Act,[†] provide fertile grounds for professionals debating both "abuse" and "normative" behaviour in the fields of child health, welfare and development and parenting in the latter part of the 20th century.

In particular, the focus on predicting possible *future* harm and a parent's *capacity* to change and thus, an increase in the use of risk assessments in preparation of future care and contact plans, have made a considerable contribution to a shift in the type of evidence filed in proceedings. The law itself demands that both diagnostic and predictive considerations are undertaken. The "diagnostic" requirement is not new** although it now has a more explicit focus. But the focus on assessing the likelihood of future harm and the necessary predictive exercise is a new development, and one which arguably does require particular expertise.

A common feature of discussions about the increased use of expertise beyond those of social workers is whether all this expert evidence is necessary. It is not possible, on the basis of the survey data on cases, to say precisely how much of this new evidence augments existing social work evidence, how much of it is replacing traditional social work evidence, and what proportion constitutes additional evidence. Indeed, in the area of family assessments in particular, it appears that the question itself is increasingly in need of reframing. The boundaries are not always as clear or as predictable as is sometimes suggested. This has become the case for several reasons.

First, as outlined above, the law itself now requires professionals to focus both on existing harms, or their likelihood, and on future possibilities, of both harm to children and of changes in parenting behaviours. This focus has become increasingly important, partly because research continues to demonstrate that there are also risks attached to placing children in care,[††] and partly because of the impact on professionals of a powerful underlying philosophy in child protection, namely, that in most cases, children are best brought up by their parents. Thus, notwithstanding a finding of current harm to children, professionals also need the best available knowledge about the

* See Bates & Brophy, *The Appliance of Science? The Use of Expert Evidence in Child Care Proceedings* (forthcoming) .

† "Harm" means ill treatment or the impairment of health or development; "development" means physical, intellectual, emotional, social or behavioural development; "health" means physical or mental health; "ill treatment" includes sexual abuse and forms of ill treatment which are not physical (Children Act 1989 s 31(9)).

** For example, under the previous legislation, an assessment of proper development, health and ill-treatment was necessary to meet the requirement of s.1(b)(i) of the Children and Young Persons Act 1969.

†† For example, evidence of lack of stability of placement of children with substitute families following care orders continues to raise considerable concerns (see Millham Bullock, Hosie and Haak, *Lost in Care: The problem of maintaining links between children in care and their families*, (1986) Gower).

future risks which parents may represent to their children, about the capacity of parents to change, and about the timescale in which that change might be achieved. Arguably, it is in this area that experts in the field of child and family welfare can offer some important "added value" in the context of evidence-based practice.

This exercise, however, has undoubtedly added to what, in some cases, were already "grey" and sometimes overlapping boundaries between the assessments undertaken by different specialists. There are, for example, *some* common functions between the tasks undertaken by senior social workers undertaking a comprehensive assessment,[*] and those undertaken by a child and adolescent psychiatrist during a psychiatric family assessment.[†] Thus, although certain experts instructed in care proceedings may inevitably retread *some* of the ground previously addressed by social workers, few consultants would take it as "read"; arguably all would wish to retrace those steps to formulate their own assessment and recommendations. That exercise is inevitable and is, in part, probably also a consequence of the currently fragmented approach to the provision of child and family mental health services in the field of child protection.[**] However, it can also operate to safeguard the interests of children and families where it is likely children will be placed in the public care system.

In some cases, a comprehensive social work assessment (the "orange" book assessment) will have been undertaken; in others, it may not. The reasons why it may not have been undertaken, however, are complex and cannot be generalised on the basis of these data,[††] but several factors emerging from the project appear important. There is some limited evidence to suggest that such assessments are only being undertaken in the context of legal proceedings. There may be good reasons for this. For example, it may be the case that in the absence of proceedings, parents would simply not agree to an assessment. The role of legal proceedings in focusing the minds of all concerned cannot be underestimated. In addition, limited resources within local authorities may also have made a contribution.

Whatever the reasons, two important factors arise from this development. First, in certain types of assessments, for example, those involving an assessment of parenting skills undertaken in the context of a multi-disciplinary assessment, or by certain types of family centres[***] (or residential centres), parents attend a number of sessions. The focus of work is on intervention, feedback and support aimed, not surprisingly, at achieving a change in parenting behaviours. Thus, a "forensic" exercise and the treatment process can run concurrently.

Second, local authority care plans and contact arrangements increasingly depend on the assessment and views of these specialists. Thus, one further consequence of this shift towards expert assessments in the context of legal proceedings is that final planning often does not take place until some time after the instigation of court proceedings. This has particular and worrying consequences for the position of parents, and these are discussed elsewhere.[†††]

b) Changes to legal procedures

Two further changes to law and legal procedure are important. First, the movement from largely oral to written evidence. Second, the requirement that, regardless of content, *all* expert evidence is filed, and it is filed *prior* to the final hearing.[*] These two features have had a considerable impact. Such attempts to make all the issues more transparent at a much earlier stage in the proceedings also reveals the substantial underlying complexities within

* See, DoH (1988) *Protecting Children: A Guide for Social Workers undertaking a Comprehensive Assessment.*

† For example, both professionals will address issues associated with "dangerousness", children's needs and parents' perceptions of those needs, routine patterns of care provided for children, the profile of parents/carers and early family history and current family composition. Equally, personality and attitude form a common feature of both types of assessments. In certain instances, the psychiatrist will explore mental health issues – issues which have often already been identified by social workers.

** It should be remembered that publication of *A Guide for Social Workers undertaking a Comprehensive Assessment* (DoH, 1988) was published three years before the introduction of the Children Act 1989, which took effect in 1991.

†† Guidance on this issue indicates that such an assessment is likely to be needed where a child has been removed from home and care proceedings are being instituted, or where a child is already subject to a care order and decisions about their future need to be made, or where there are professional concerns about parental care but no incident has occurred to spark off an initial investigation, or where there is a history of professional involvement with a family but there are no improvements in parental care and professionals feel 'stuck' (DoH, 1988, para 6.3, p.20).

*** i.e. those designated under DoH (1991b) *The Children Act 1989, Guidance & Regulations, Vol 2 (Family Support Day Care and Educational Provision for Young Children)* as incorporating a therapeutic aim where the focus is on intensive work with families experiencing severe difficulties to bring about improvements in family functioning.

††† See Brophy & Bates,(1998), *The Position of Parents using Experts in Care Proceedings: A failure of Partnership?*

many cases. These complexities, arguably always present in care proceedings, not only now become apparent much earlier in proceedings, but importantly, they are now available in a "concrete" form and to all parties, in particular, to parents. That is clearly a benefit over previous proceedings, but it also has a number of consequences. As indicated above, a failure (for whatever reason) in the early stages of cases, to spell out with sufficient precision the issues at stake, means that some or indeed all of that sifting and assessment exercise is increasingly being undertaken by child welfare specialists, predominantly those in the field of child and adolescent psychiatry.

c)   Lack of confidence in social work skills and expertise

Alongside these substantial changes to law and legal procedures, two further factors are important. First, there has been a fairly widespread lack of confidence by courts in social work skills and expertise. This lack of confidence is perhaps coupled with some confusion about both the boundaries and the overlap between the skills of social workers and others. But it is also informed by the variation in skills and expertise of social workers involved in care proceedings. It is likely to have had a number of consequences for the practices of both guardians and local authorities. It may have led some local authorities – or their legal services departments – to err on the side of caution and seek expert assessments to augment existing social work evidence where, in practice, the expert adds very little other than "authority and status". However, from the perspective of parties and in the context of "winning" cases under the current system, in a climate of widespread lack of confidence in social work skills and expertise, that contribution cannot be ignored.

The court's lack of confidence in social work skills has contributed to an increase in guardians' own use of experts: 41 per cent of guardians in the survey identified this issue as *one* of the reasons for their own increased use. This course of action by guardians could arguably be seen as yet further undermining social work skills. It could be argued that in a limited number of cases, guardians should be more willing to challenge practices, such as the unnecessary use of experts, which contribute to that decline. However, this also raises the question of the most appropriate arena in which to locate that challenge. Individual cases may not be the most appropriate place to challenge what is now a national shift in the character of most care proceedings.[†] A strategic approach should be mounted on a number of fronts. To be effective, this issue should be taken up in local and national policy forums, for example, at a local level in local authorities, in the forum for decision making between legal services and social services, and by courts in the Family Court Business Committees and in the Family Court Forums. This would mean that magistrates and clerks in family proceedings courts and district judges in care centres are aware of, and sympathetic towards, an *appropriate* challenge by a guardian in which he or she seeks to mount an argument for proceeding on the basis of social work evidence only.

For such an approach to be successful, however, social work skills, expertise and practices in the assessment of children and families need to be of high quality and they need to be consistently applied. Early identification of the issues at stake through a proper assessment, and sufficient precision in the type and content of expert assessment, where these are required, are important. At the present time, one important gap in information relates to decision making within local authorities where they seek expert assessments, particularly child and family psychiatric assessments. In the survey, for those cases in which only the local authority sought expert assessments, in almost all cases the guardian supported that decision. However, what we do not

* See, for example, *Oxford CC v M [1994]* 1 FCR 753.

† We say this because it may not be in the best interests of the particular child to confront practices in this way and risk both delay and censure.

know from these data is whether the guardian supported the decision because the case demanded expertise and skills beyond the boundaries of social work expertise, or whether the particular local authority, for whatever reason, was unable to ensure the necessary work and assessments were undertaken by social workers. This is an area which requires further investigation; however, care should be taken to ensure that practices in a minority of cases do not determine any short-term changes to policy in this field.

d) *The use of child and adolescent psychiatrists*

The second important feature of care proceedings involving experts is the high use of child and adolescent psychiatrists by both the local authority and the guardian. The existence of concerns about mental health issues and the need for a diagnosis of mental health states appears to underscore recourse to experts by many guardians: 57 per cent identified this as one reason for their own increased use. Three issues arise from this finding. First, it leaves a substantial proportion of guardians whose reasons for increasing their own use of experts did *not* include a need for a mental health diagnosis, even though, as the survey demonstrates, child and adolescent psychiatrists were the dominant specialists commissioned by guardians. It may be the case that there is an element of confusion about areas of expertise between, for example, child and adolescent psychiatrists and clinical child psychologists. In matters of attachment, adequate parenting and emotional development there is some overlap. Choice, however, may also be largely dependent on who is available locally. Status factors may also play a large part as consultant psychiatrists are seen as carrying more weight in court.

Second, the high use of child and adolescent psychiatrists may also indicate an element of late planning and consequently the late involvement of experts in cases. Evidence on the sequencing of court leaves (i.e. permission) for expert examination or assessment indicates that, in most cases, proceedings have progressed some way before the guardian seeks leave for an expert assessment – they are not usually the first party to seek leave.* There are often good reasons for this. For example, an assessment initiated by the local authority may be underway, or the authority may have obtained leave at the first directions hearing to obtain an assessment. However, the survey shows that in just over a third of those cases where the guardian was the *only* party seeking expert assessments, they did so to obtain an assessment of a child's development. This is arguably a need which should have become apparent and been addressed by the local authority much earlier in proceedings.†

Moreover, in the same sub-sample of cases (where only the guardian sought expert evidence), just over a third of guardians indicated that they had obtained expert evidence which should have been obtained by the local authority. The survey highlights several issues which may underscore this trend. Overall, guardians did not express a high level of satisfaction with local child and family mental health services. It is also likely to be the case that, in the context of legal proceedings, local authorities are also dissatisfied with such services. Also, guardians have a wider choice of experts from which they can select, and they are more likely to select specialists with a considerable track record as expert witnesses in public law proceedings. Thus, it may be a "strategic" decision on the part of some local authorities to proceed in the absence of certain evidence in the knowledge that this will eventually be addressed by the guardian who has an unrestricted access to a range of highly experienced clinicians. There are also considerable financial reasons for this approach. If the guardian instructs the expert, the costs are met by the Legal Aid Board. Further

* See Brophy & Bates (1998)

† It should be noted, however, that part of the explanation in such instances may have been parents' refusal to co-operate with assessments and hence, the need for court proceedings.

research should address this issue but again, it should be emphasised that practices in a relatively small number of local authorities should not over-determine policy developments in this field.

It is also important to look at some of the implications of this apparent shift of responsibility for obtaining the necessary assessments from a minority of local authorities to guardians. It can add to a lack of early planning and identification of issues, and this can become part of the justification for the use of experts. Once a court application is made, the guardian gets caught up in that process. The lack of early attention to these issues, coupled with the lack of confidence by courts in social work skills and expertise, may mean that guardians are less inclined to address these issues with local authorities and more likely to take a pragmatic approach and instruct an expert to undertake some or all of that work. It is likely much will depend on what the guardian considers achievable by the particular local authority,* and what the guardian considers to be in the best interests of the relevant child or children at this stage in proceedings.

Child and adolescent mental health services

a) *Matching service needs with service providers*

Despite the clear need to bring more expert knowledge to bear on crucial decisions about the future care and wellbeing of very vulnerable children, the survey shows that the shift towards using experts in proceedings has not been matched by significant changes in the willingness and availability of many local child and family mental health services to provide the necessary services. For example, most guardians (72 per cent) reported that local services had no resources or commitment to undertake further therapeutic work if that was necessary.

This is an important finding when placed in the context of the Children Act philosophy characterised by support for parenthood and "partnership" between parents and the state in the care of children, and coupled with a commitment to multidisciplinary interagency co-operation. Although the reasons underlying this apparent failure on the part of many local child and adolescent mental health services are complex and require further investigation,† indications are that, in many instances, assessments and reports for public law proceedings fall outside of current contractual NHS obligations.

The improvements required by guardians in local child and family mental health services focused on both resources and training: services required more resources but, in addition, specialists within services required specific training with regard to providing assessments and reports for public law proceedings. Clearly, any discussion about the inability of some local child and adolescent mental health services to meet the needs posed by care proceedings has to be set within a more general discussion of the development of community mental health services (see Sepping, 1992; Trowell, 1991; ADSS/Royal College of Psychiatry, 1993).

The current lack of provision and confidence in many local CAMHS has had a number of effects. First, perhaps because relatively few guardians were satisfied with the provision of local child and family mental health services, "locality" was not a consideration which came very high in their selection criteria when appointing experts.** Second, as the data indicate, because guardians are not geographically constrained when choosing experts, they are more likely to instruct "national" experts rather than specialists working in locally based services. These "national" experts may be more likely to be

* It may be the case that the guardian is well aware that neither the local authority nor the local mental health services can provide the necessary assessments and thus, in taking on the responsibility for obtaining those assessments elsewhere, the guardian is acting in the best interests of the particular child or children.

† Some of these issues are further pursued in Stage III of the project during interviews with a sample of experts (see Brophy, Brown, Cohen and Radcliffe, *Law and Medicine: Psychiatry at the Interface of Child Protection Litigation*).

** This suggestion has been confirmed by Stage III of the project. For example, with regard to instructing child and adolescent psychiatrists, guardians on certain panels tend to use "national" figures located in specialist teaching hospitals/centres rather than specialists within local child and adolescent mental health services. And in some areas, there does not appear to be a local service which can provide *any* expertise for this type of work.

retired or semi-retired from the NHS, or be located in research/teaching hospitals with an international reputation.

As discussed above, this issue, combined with the guardian's easier and/or quicker access to funding, has in some limited instances, resulted in the guardian rather than the local authority commissioning experts. Further research is needed on the decision-making processes between the guardian and the local authority for that group of cases where guardians are seeking evidence which, in their view, should be obtained by the local authority. However, again it should be noted this development is by no means a national phenomenon. It is likely, for example, that GALRO panels within the catchment area of leading teaching/research institutions may be less exposed to pressures to "replace" the work of the local authority as the expertise in such institutions *may* be available to both the local authority and the guardian.*

Thirdly, guardians' selection criteria centre on the *experienced* expert witness. In practice this means someone with a sympathy for, and an understanding of, the particular needs of children and parents in legal proceedings, and experience of providing evidence for those proceedings. This applies to the selection of both psychologists and psychiatrists.

A strong preference for the legally experienced/Children Act literate clinician may also have had an impact on experts and the shaping of services. A relatively small number of "national" expert witnesses in the field of child protection have clearly built up an area of skills and expertise in the legal arena, particularly since the instigation of the Children Act. In certain respects, this sets them apart from some clinicians working in local services. At one level, this increasingly specialised, legally experienced group works well, at least for guardians. As the survey demonstrates, most guardians, not surprisingly, are satisfied with the work undertaken by these experts. But for some local authorities – and perhaps many parents – this development into a "two tier" system does not work so well.

Fourthly, this concentration of skills and expertise in a relatively small group of people, while clearly meeting the requirements of guardians and the needs of those children they represent, can nevertheless create a number of problems for clinicians and those responsible for the provision of local community mental health services within the NHS. Evidence suggests that it is leading to an overload of specific categories of experts. This is especially so in the field of child and adolescent psychiatry where there is a very limited number of specialists who are able/willing to undertake this type of work.[†] Notwithstanding the contractual problems in providing such services, a strong preference for the experienced expert witness presents problems for newly qualified consultants or senior registrars wishing to gain experience in the legal arena: they are not appointed because they lack experience – they lack experience because parties will not appoint them.

b) The new legal agenda and the implications for clinicians

Despite indications of a shortage of experienced experts, relatively few guardians reported actually failing to appoint an expert in the field of either psychiatry or psychology. However, from the survey data, we cannot identify how long guardians were able or willing to wait for the expert of their choice.** As outlined above, the implications are that there remains a limited pool of specialists undertaking this category of work. From guardians' experiences, the reasons why the pool of "willing *and* able" expertise is not as wide as the total pool of specialists in the community are, in part, resource-based (some services are already reported as being overstretched),

* Although this may, for example, depend on whether the hospital trust in which a particular consultant is employed is contracted to supply this category of work to a local authority.

† For example, at mid April 1996, the number of consultant child and adolescent psychiatrists (based on registrations with The Royal College of Psychiatry) was put at 345. This figure may well under-estimate the total population since consultants are not obliged to register with the Royal College. Equally, not all consultants are employed within the regional health authorities in England and Wales and local lists would not include retired consultants who continue to work privately. Whatever the total potential pool of experts, as we indicate above, not all of these are able/willing to undertake assessments for the purposes of legal proceedings – the *Directory of Expert Witnesses* (1996) produced by the Law Society, for example, lists just 19 consultant child and adolescent psychiatrists whose specialist areas include those likely to be addressed in public law proceedings (i.e. child abuse, neglect, contact issues).

** This issue is pursued further in interviews with guardians in Stage II of the project, see Brophy and Bates (1999).

but some experts continue to express a dislike of the adversarial nature of public law proceedings. In addition, some experts have expressed a lack of conviction about the validity of this type of work. For example, some feel they can frequently only state the obvious.

Thus, many of the traditional reasons why some experts disliked "court work" remain. But there are some new reasons for resisting or refusing referrals. Care cases are taking longer, there are now more issues to be considered, joint instructions can make the exercise considerably more complex,* and reports are expected to conform to a particular format and style. In addition, where there are conflicts between experts, they are now expected to meet prior to the final hearing and construct statements of agreement or disagreement for the court.† Equally, there are suggestions that experts should consider alternative perspectives and available research in their reports (see below).

In other words, "law" is setting out a new agenda for child welfare specialists and for referring parties. In theory, if not in practice, the days of, 'Here are the papers, Please tell us what you think,' are over. Court directions with regard to the use of experts, both to advocates seeking leave to instruct experts, and with regard to letters of instructions to experts now aim to make the reasons for the referral more transparent to *all* parties and to specify the questions to be addressed to the expert.** Equally, the duties and responsibilities of experts have been clearly defined.††

For some specialists, for example, those who work on a national basis and spend a substantial proportion of their time undertaking assessments, writing reports and giving evidence in courts, the new agenda is perhaps well understood. This is partly because this group of specialists is, in effect, contributing to that new agenda both by their work in court and by their academic writing and research. However, for some clinicians in local services (e.g. child guidance clinics) where contractual obligations do not necessarily cover this type of work and where general practice, training and priorities are much less geared towards public law demands, the new agenda – whereby "law" is, in effect, attempting to carve out a job specification for child welfare specialists – may provide additional reasons for rejecting this type of work. Taken in the context of those local child and family adolescent health services which are already over-stretched, it is not, perhaps, surprising that there is resistance to undertaking this type of assessment work in many locally based services.

Cases in the survey

a)   *Directions in the family proceedings courts*

Although most cases involving experts are likely to be transferred to a higher court – 53 per cent of the sample cases were transferred – a substantial number of cases involving experts are completed in the family proceedings court. Moreover, even for those cases which are ultimately transferred, evidence suggests*** that much of the expert evidence filed is likely to have been based on leave granted in the family proceedings court. This survey and the court-based study therefore highlight the importance of attention to strategies in case management at the very beginning of a case: the first directions hearing where leave is sought to instruct an expert.

Findings from the court-based study and from this survey also identify that it is usually the local authority which obtains the first, and arguably most crucial leave (i.e. permission) which allows for a child to be assessed/ examined by an expert instructed by the local authority. Moreover, the court-

* For example, more questions may be asked of the expert and some experts have referred to joint instructions as containing an impossible shopping list of questions demanding expertise more in line with "crystal ball gazing".

† *Re C* (Expert Evidence: Disclosure Practice) [1995] 1 FLR 204.

** *Re M* (Minors) (Care Proceedings: Child's Wishes) [1994] 1 FLR 794; *Re I and E* (Proceedings: Conflicting Interests) [1995] 1 FLR 581.

†† *Re AB* (A Minor) (Child Abuse: Expert Witnesses) [1995] 1 FLR 181; and CAAC, *Annual Report*, 1994/5:26.

*** Bates and Brophy, forthcoming.

based study identified that leave was usually granted at the first directions hearing.

Two points arise from this finding: First, it is essential that the guardian is present at this first hearing, and that is not always achievable. Thus, the process of commissioning expert evidence can begin in the family proceedings court without the court having the benefit of advice and input from the guardian. Whilst the need to avoid delay by getting any necessary assessments underway is understandably uppermost in the minds of professionals who attend that first hearing, it can mean that the guardian is, in effect, faced with a *fait accompli* on a number of levels. Some of these are to do with substantive questions which need to be addressed, but some are concerned with case planning and strategy. For example, it may be that he or she does not agree with the type/extent of assessment requested or with the choice of expert. It may be that he or she does not think it is actually necessary as it may not add anything of significance to existing evidence. But leaves granted at a hearing at which the guardian is not present also mean that he or she cannot exert control over strategic matters.

The second point about the first directions hearing appointment where the guardian is present relates to the guardian's confidence and willingness, if necessary, to advise the court to withhold leave at that stage. Again, because of the focus on avoiding delay, court clerks and magistrates are anxious to hasten proceedings by getting any necessary expert assessments underway. The local authority may be ready at the first hearing with a request for leave to instruct an expert. But the guardian may not have had an opportunity to come to an *informed* opinion about need, content, choice or indeed instructing strategy. In these circumstances, it may be difficult for a guardian to be assertive in his or her case management and advise the court to delay the decision until he or she has reached an informed a view. However, several findings from the project identify why that approach may have long-term benefits for cases. For example, it may reduce the number of experts and thus help reduce the overall length of cases. It may contribute to reducing *some* of the late applications for leave by parents if they are consulted at the very beginning of a case about other parties' plans with regard to the use of experts. It may also alert parents' solicitors to the need to be more fully involved in the process right at the beginning of proceedings. In other words, a short delay at the beginning of a case may have substantial benefits for the overall length and management of cases.

Two issues are, therefore, important for more effective case management. The first directions hearing is clearly crucial in determining the tone and future character of proceedings. This is where the most important decisions about the use of experts are sanctioned. Therefore, courts should not grant leave for assessments where the guardian is not present. Indeed, except in exceptional circumstances, all parties should be present at this hearing if leave is being sought for an assessment of a child/family. Second, guardians should be more pro-active at that initial appointment. If necessary, this may mean withstanding the pressures within courts on fast "throughput" and instead, advising the court to delay granting leave until the guardian has had sufficient time to ascertain whether an application for expert assessment is appropriate and the best methods of obtaining that evidence.

b) The overall duration of cases and the transfer decision

Delay in public law cases remains a dominant cause of concern and a recent report continues to highlight the range of issues likely to cause delay in cases (The Booth Report, 1996).* In this survey, the transfer decision was the main explanatory variable in understanding the duration of cases. There are a

* Avoiding Delay in Children Act Cases (1996), Dame Margaret Booth, The Lord Chancellor's Department.

number of further factors to be taken into account when looking at the impact of transfer on case duration. One important factor discussed earlier is whether anything is actually happening during the period between the decision to transfer and a first hearing in a higher court. In this sample it may be that assessments were being undertaken. Equally, it may also have been the case that for some, assessments were in fact complete and the interval was simply waiting time. Whatever the explanation, cases which started in the family proceedings court and were transferred to a care centre took an extra three months to complete; cases transferred to the High Court took an extra four and a half months to complete; cases which started in a care centre and were transferred to the High Court took an extra three months compared with the baseline group.

The Booth Report (1996) highlights one of the problems surrounding transfer: the lack of attention to ascertaining the earliest date available in the county court. However, to date no recommendations have been made in relation to reducing the waiting period or, more importantly, setting target deadlines. Given the impact on case duration of a decision to transfer to a higher court, it now seems appropriate in the interests of children and families that courts should offer a more co-ordinated service and therefore set a maximum waiting period considered acceptable.

A considerable amount of training and research has focused on the role of professionals involved in the care and protection of young children at risk – both during investigations, throughout legal proceedings and following a court order. Co-operation, co-ordination and partnership are now key concepts in policy development. Multiagency co-operation and multidisciplinary education have dominated policy debate in this field. It is therefore appropriate that the administration of courts should be part of that exercise. Changing courts need not equate with delay in a co-ordinated service which is focused on the needs of children and families. In principle, a co-ordinated court service could, for example, allow for the family proceedings court not only to make the transfer decision, but in addition, and at the same time, set a date for the next directions hearing in the care centre.*

The practices of professionals and institutions

a) Cases in which one party only filed expert reports

In those cases in the survey where one party only filed expert reports (the local authority or guardian) with regard to the local authority, the dominant reports came from paediatricians, child and adolescent psychiatrists and independent social work reports based on parenting skills assessments.† With regard to the expert reports filed by guardians, child and adolescent psychiatric reports were the major form of evidence.

In most cases expert reports were based on sole instructions. In such cases, although both the local authority and the guardians consulted with each other and *some* parents when experts were commissioned, each professional was less likely to consult with parents about both the need for, and choice of, a specific expert.

In both types of cases, that is, those in which only the local authority instructed experts and those in which only the guardian instructed experts, courts did not take a pro-active role in seeking the inclusion of other parties in instructions to experts. Given the small number of cases in which any degree of joint instructions of experts was indicated, the relatively low level

* A similar process now permits magistrates' courts to schedule the first plea and directions hearing in the Crown Court.

† For example, those undertaken at specialist family centres.

of consultation which professionals undertook with parents is worrying. This is especially so when posed against notions of "partnership" and consultation with parents in the care of their children.

As others have subsequently argued (DoH, 1995), the instigation of legal proceedings may change the nature of partnership but such proceedings should not necessarily mark the termination of attempts to work with parents. Indeed, as argued above, since the expectation is that following a care order a local authority should try to work in partnership with parents, the approach taken *during* proceedings remains important. Much, however, may depend on the nature of the allegations and it may not be possible or appropriate to engage some parents either in consultations about the use of experts or in joint instructions. One albeit controversial example is where there are allegations of sexual abuse.* Nevertheless, when considering the position of a non-abusing parent and where joint instructions are not possible, information and consultation with regard to the use of experts may prove beneficial to both child and parent whatever the outcome of a case.† This will include whether the decision is to attempt to rebuild a safe environment for a child's return or long-term or permanent removal. Such an approach, while falling short of the "partnership" ideal, nevertheless indicates the importance of encouraging continued participation and involvement of parents whenever possible.

Courts have not been pro-active in encouraging parties to seek joint instructions; most experts are instructed by one party and the local authority and the guardian did not consult with all parents about the need for expert assessment or the choice of expert. Taken together, these findings point to the need for closer scrutiny and management of early directions hearings. This cannot be achieved unless (a) the guardian attends, and (b) leave is withheld until he or she has sufficient information to give the court *informed* advice on how to proceed with regard to directions for expert assessments. Courts will not necessarily know if professionals have consulted with parents. Evidence indicates that parents' legal representatives are unlikely to be pro-active during the early stages in proceedings.** Guardians have a duty to ascertain the substantive issues which require the assessment of an expert and a duty to ascertain the views of parents, but they could also take a more pro-active role in the strategic planning of cases and advising the court about what is likely to be achievable.

Some guardians are already undertaking this work but practices vary considerably. Courts can support guardians in this respect by refusing leave unless the guardian is present, by withholding leave until the guardian is ready to give *informed* advice, and by checking that cross-party consultations have taken place and, in particular, that parents' views have been ascertained.

Cases in which the guardian was the *only party* to file any expert reports accounted for 17 per cent of the sample cases. Received wisdom has suggested that the increase in use of experts by guardians is, in part, due to local authorities looking to guardians to provide evidence which they themselves should provide.†† As outlined above, although the survey found some evidence for this (about one third of guardians in this sub-sample identified this to be the case), most did not consider they had commissioned evidence which should have been obtained by a local authority.

In most cases where the guardian was the only party to file any expert reports this was done "by agreement" with other parties, mostly with the local authority but also, in some cases, parents. It is not, however, possible from the survey data to determine precisely what this meant in practice. It *could,* for example, mean that the specific issues to be addressed by the

* Views may be divided on this. For example, some practitioners hold the view that partnership is not possible because of the characteristics frequently identified with sexual abuse such as the addictive nature of sexual abuse, the strategies which sexual abusers use to manipulate and intimidate children and partners, and because of the extent to which sexual abusers minimise and deny the extent of their offending. As has subsequently been pointed out (DoH, 1995:78/79) negotiations will have to address the nature of allegations, the wishes of the child, and strengths and attitude of the non-abusing parent.

† Other writers have also developed the concept of partnership in this regard, see, for example, Tunnard, 1991 and Thoburn, Lewis and Shemmings, 1998.

** See Brophy and Bates (1998).

†† That is, evidence necessary to meet the first threshold criteria under s.31(2) of The Children Act.

expert and the particular expert to be appointed were agreed, in which case perhaps there is little to chose between these cases and what might constitute a joint appointment. However, since guardians *also* identified that the reports in these cases were *not* actually based on joint instructions, it is more likely that it was simply agreed that the guardian would instruct an expert, possibly because of his or her wider choice of experts and easier access to funding. It remains a question, therefore, as to why joint instructions were not possible in these cases and why courts made no attempts to encourage the guardian to seek a joint instruction.

As indicated above, in most of these cases the survey indicated that the guardian had mostly consulted with the local authority about the choice of a specific expert but had consulted with parents in under a third of cases. Given the guardians' wider access to "national" experts and the relatively low level of satisfaction identified with child and adolescent mental health services, it is perhaps unlikely that his or her choice would be opposed by local authorities. The same may may not, however, be true for parents. Certain experts are identified with holding specific views, for example, with regard to views about contact and rehabilitation of children in cases of alleged abuse. Unless parents are consulted where it is possible and appropriate about who specifically should be appointed, they are likely to become further alienated from both the legal process and the professionals. This, amongst other factors, may have an impact on the response of parents to the professionals in proceedings, the views and recommendations of experts, and the willingness of parents to participate in future plans for the children.*

b) Cases in which more than one party filed expert reports

Over half the cases (65 per cent) in this sub-sample contained reports which focused on the same issues/concerns addressed in a previous report. For some children (31 per cent), this resulted in more than one *face-to-face* examination or assessment.

i) The "hired gun" syndrome and experts appointed by parents

A common theme in discussions about the use of experts in care proceedings has been that many experts appointed by parents are already known to be biased in their favour. In effect, they continue to represent the "hired gun" syndrome associated with practices prior to the Children Act. However, not all experts instructed by parents necessarily support the cause of parents. First, many expert reports filed by parents in this sub-sample (38 per cent) did not, in fact, address the question of the most appropriate order in a case. Where they did, the proportions of those who supported or opposed the order sought by a local authority were similar (23 per cent and 25 per cent respectively). In other words, the notion that experts acting for parents are simply "hired guns" is not supported by these data.

Second, in those cases where experts appointed by parents had addressed the same issues/concerns as a previous report, only 18 per cent totally disagreed with the recommendations made by a previous expert. Over 40 per cent in fact agreed with the recommendations made.†

When we compared this with the levels of agreement or disagreement between experts in cases where guardians commissioned a second report, although the number of cases in this sub-sample is smaller (79 cases compared with 170 above), the survey also showed that there was also a level of disagreement between the experts in these cases. This applied with regard to both the assessment and the appropriate recommendations. Just

---

* For this consultation process to be really effective, further changes are necessary with regard to the legal representation of parents. These issues are outlined and discussed in Brophy and Bates (1998).

† See Table 4.19 – a further 30 per cent indicated partial agreement with the recommendations made by a previous expert, the remainder were not comparable or contained no recommendations.

under a third of experts instructed by guardians disagreed with both the assessment and recommendations of a previous expert. Moreover, if cases where there was partial disagreement are included, this figure rises to over half of those cases.

In summary, it is not simply experts appointed by parents who disagree about issues, there is evidence of a divergence of views between experts appointed by guardians and those appointed by local authorities. That experts disagree over the most appropriate recommendations to make in a case and the fact that disagreement is not *necessarily* dependent on which party instructs them is an important finding. It has several implications. First, it supports the views of guardians in the survey that due to the new threshold criteria and the focus on predicting future harms and a parent's capacity to change, cases are often very complex. Experts may come to different conclusions when addressing the same set of circumstances and perhaps the same questions. They may agree about past events; they may also agree that a care order is necessary; but future plans and placements can, nevertheless, be a point of considerable disagreement. Second, given that experts register a degree of disagreement about the appropriate future course of action, what are the implications for future policy with regard to the current focus on joint instructions? We address these issues below.

ii)   Competing paradigms make complex cases

Since the introduction of the Children Act, the debate on instructing experts in care proceedings has focused increasingly on the advantages of joint instructions. Perceptions of the proliferation of expert evidence have given rise to criticisms based on the high cost of experts, delay, duplication of evidence and overloading of some experts. Some guardians have also expressed difficulties in assessing competing reports. For example, should equal weight be given to a report based on an observation of a child compared with a report based on an "interactive" interview with a child? Joint instructions to a single expert has been seen as the solution to a considerable range of financial and practical problems.

However, little discussion has focused on the benefits of more information, or on problems of ensuring that the full range of available child welfare knowledge is made available to courts. We lack data on the full range of differences between experts addressing the same issues. The survey identified that a considerable degree of difference existed between experts addressing the same issues and concerns, resulting in different recommendations being made. What we do not know is the magnitude of differences and how these are underscored by both clinical judgement and experience and the best available research evidence.

iii)   Competing expert evidence and future policy

One question which these data raise is that if the preferred trend in this field is towards joint instructions of a single expert, how will that change ensure that the best available child welfare knowledge remains available to the court? Will the reports of appointed experts reflect both their own clinical views and judgements *and* those of different schools of thought? Limited data to date suggest that experts do not routinely use research findings or other perspectives in their reports for courts. Some experts have questioned whether it is appropriate for them to undertake that exercise; they do not see it as part of their responsibility to assess the available research evidence or to present the views or perspectives of other clinicians.

We do not know how widespread this view is amongst experts currently providing reports for courts. Some practitioners increasingly argue that evidence-based medicine is about integrating individual clinical expertise with the best external evidence from systematic research.* At the level of individual decision making in legal proceedings, the role of research is viewed as, at least, problematic. General principles derived from research may not be seen as especially helpful although views are divided on this.†

The use of research also raises questions about how to assess its comprehensiveness, validity and relevance, and indeed about whose responsibility it is to undertake that exercise. Nevertheless, if decisions are to be informed by the best available child welfare knowledge, it is important to keep two factors to the forefront. First, child welfare knowledge is not a uniform category. Second, that lack of uniformity may be a positive characteristic. Human behaviour is immensely complex and subject to individual and environmental influences. The dialectic process of scientific research and writing allows for continual assessment and re-assessment in understanding, explaining and, if necessary, "treating" certain behaviours. The existing body of child welfare knowledge is thus neither static nor uniform. If decisions concerning the future care and welfare of children are going to benefit from this developing body of knowledge, mechanisms should be retained which allow for the full breadth of available knowledge, alternative perspectives and systematic research to be available to the court. Solutions which, in effect, limit this information may serve the needs and concerns of professionals for speed and simplicity. However, such an approach will not necessarily ensure that a more informed exploration of the issues and available options is undertaken. Limiting the range of child welfare knowledge which reaches the legal arena may have an effect on the quality of final decision making and may limit the options available to courts when considering the future care of some children. This caution applies to a range of solutions currently posed in this field, for example, the possibility of restricting the use of experts through the development of a system of court appointed experts.** The same is true of joint instructions if involvement in such instructions would remove or reduce a party's right to question the subsequent report and, if necessary, seek a second opinion.

These developments also raise questions for the future role and work of the guardian. For example, the survey indicates that in selecting experts, the previous skills and courtroom experience of a known and trusted expert dominate the selection criteria. Whether such experts used research findings in reports did not rate highly as a criterion for their appointment by guardians. Preliminary findings from further research indicate that the views of experts themselves on this issue vary widely.††

However, it may be the case that if trends in this field mean the expert's role and responsibility *is* to be expanded in this way but without increased services and resources, those specialists who are experienced in court work may not be willing or indeed able to continue to undertake the volume of work currently referred to them. Moreover, clinicians based in some local services may be even less willing to undertake work in this field. It also means that as advisers to the court, guardians will have to be up to date on current research in child welfare although they may not be deemed competent to judge its validity.

* See, for example, Sackett *et al*, BMJ, 1996.

† *Re R* (A Minor) (Expert's Evidence) [1991] 1 FLR, 291 (Cazalet J); but see also *Manchester v B* [1996] 1 FLR, 324. It is also the case that changes in policies with regard to the care and upbringing of children have been greatly influenced by research. For example, the whole shift in approaches to 'contact' (between children and non-custodial parents following divorce or between children and birth parents following adoption) was based on studies which addressed the well-being of children in relation to continued contact with parents.

** A move favoured by the experts but not the lawyers involved in the Expert Witness Group – see CAAC, *Annual Report,* 1993/4:15.

†† Stage III of the project – interviews with experts in Brophy *et al*, 1997.

Improving case management

The children: age and ethnicity

The survey highlights the fact that many children who are the subject of care proceedings are likely to be very young – 63 per cent of the sample were six years of age or under.

- The child's sense of timing should be taken into account when setting a target for the maximum acceptable waiting period when transferring cases from the family proceedings court to the care centre.

The majority of children were white European (84 per cent). However, the data indicate that black children and children of mixed parentage were more likely to be the subject of care applications. Thus, ethnicity remains a risk factor associated with applications under public law proceedings. However, details of children's ethnic background continue to be excluded from court application forms. This can create problems for GALRO panels in attempting to match guardians and children in terms of ethnic group even supposing panel membership is expanding in terms of diversity.

- Details of children's ethnic background should be routinely supplied to courts when applications are made so that courts and panels can ensure that, where possible, children and guardians are matched with regard to ethnic background.

- Panels need a wider range of guardians from different ethnic backgrounds.

- Existing guardians also need training and support to extend their knowledge of different patterns of family life and to increase their confidence about when and how that specific knowledge is relevant.

Although all professionals in child protection must be aware of the importance of attention to age, sex, "race", and cultural, religious and linguistic background of children, there is an assumption that contemporary methods and theories underlying approaches to family assessment are applicable across cultural boundaries. This assumption has not been adequately investigated. There are a very limited number of black child and adolescent psychiatrists and very little literature on the relationship between social problems, parenting and ethnicity.

- Further research is necessary to explore child protection litigation in the minority ethnic groups.

- There is also a need to develop training materials for guardians which translate the general principles of equal opportunities and anti-discrimination policies into meaningful knowledge and skills in the context of the guardian's role and responsibilities.

Social work skills and expertise

The lack of confidence by courts in social work skills and expertise requires urgent attention on a number of fronts.

Within local authorities

- This lack of confidence is exacerbated by the lack of early attention to the identification of the issues at stake in cases by social workers and insufficient precision in the type and focus of expert assessment necessary. It is also escalated by local authorities' commissioning experts to do family assessments in cases where arguably these should have been undertaken by the local authority.

- Attention should be given to the expertise and support offered to social workers who are involved in child protection work which result in court proceedings. Such social workers should receive training in court skills.

- Further investigation is necessary to examine the balance of power and decision making between legal services and social services when the use of experts is being considered.

By courts

- As part of a local and national strategy for the appropriate use of experts, the court's lack of confidence in social work skills and expertise should be addressed in discussions in local Family Court Business Committees and in the Family Court Forums.

- Magistrates, clerks, and judges should be aware of, and sympathetic towards, an *appropriate* challenge by a local authority or a guardian to an application for unnecessary use of experts.

- In certain respects, social workers are experts. However, courts will generally be more impressed with experienced senior social workers than with newly qualified field workers. Both should be accorded the same degree of rigour and courtesy as other expert witnesses. By their very nature, the judgements of social workers are particularly liable to attack under cross-examination by solicitors or barristers. In this respect, training in court skills and the rules of evidence is appropriate for *all* social workers involved in care proceedings.

- During hearings where social workers are present they should not be relegated to seats at the back of the court or away from committee type seating arrangements where other professionals such as the guardian, the clerk and the advocates sit. Seating should facilitate consultation between the social workers and the local authority's legal representative.

By guardians

- Guardians should be more pro-active in challenging the inappropriate use of experts by local authorities. They should be less willing to use experts for assessments which they, as social workers, should be competent to undertake.

- Professional support should be more widely available to guardians.

Assessing children and families: which expert?

Some confusion may exist about areas of expertise between child psychiatrists and clinical child psychologists. For example, in matters of attachment, adequate parenting and emotional development, there is some overlap.

- Careful thought should be given as to whether in terms of the specific needs within a case, a clinical child psychologist might be equally appropriate and possibly more available to undertake an assessment that a child and adolescent psychiatrist.

Child and adolescent mental health services

There is an urgent need for further investigation and clarification of:

- The contractual obligations and the relationship between child and adolescent mental health service providers and local authorities social services departments.

- Individual NHS contracts within CAMHS.

- Assessments and reports for court proceedings should be seen as an essential part of the system of family support which community mental health services are contracted to supply. Individual contracts for the full range of staff, including psychologists and psychiatric social workers working in multidisciplinary teams should incorporate and not exclude this type of work. In many areas, it appears that multidisplinary teams are a thing of the past.

- In the short term, in-service training should address the necessary skills, expertise and knowledge required for assessing children and families in public law proceedings.

- Where issues of the independence of experts are raised, reciprocal arrangements between service providers across geographical boundaries should be possible.

Directions hearings/appointments

Courts and guardians should be more pro-active at early directions hearings and this is especially the case at the very first directions hearing.

- Courts should not grant leave for an expert assessment in the absence of the guardian. Except in exceptional circumstances, all parties should be present at the first hearing at which leave is granted for an assessment of a child and family.

- Where necessary, the guardian should be more pro-active in delaying applications for leave until he or she has had sufficient time to ascertain both substantive and strategic issues with other parties.

Delay in cases

A considerable amount of attention has been given to the role of transfer in extending the length of cases. It is now important that attention be given to the waiting time between courts.

- Targets should be set giving the maximum waiting period considered acceptable. These targets should take into consideration the very young age of many children involved in these proceedings.

- Court services should aim to provide a co-ordinated service. Changing courts following a transfer decision need not equate with delay. It should be possible for the family proceedings courts not only to make the transfer decision but simultaneously to set a date for the next directions hearing in the care centre.

"Partnership" in the context of court proceedings

Court proceedings currently represent a gap in this policy objective. While there are certain circumstances where this ideal is not achievable, in principle, proceedings should not mark the end of attempts to work with parents, to consult them, and to provide them with information.

- Except in exceptional circumstances, professionals should be under a specific duty to consult with parents about both the need for and the choice of an expert to undertake a child and family psychiatric assessment and/or experts to undertake an assessment of their parenting skills and capacities.

- Guardians should ensure that this consultation exercise has been undertaken prior to leave being granted.

- Courts should ascertain that this exercise has been undertaken before granting leave.

For this consultation process to be effective, however, parents require a higher standard of legal representation. Further research (Brophy and Bates, 1998) demonstrates that they are currently at a considerable disadvantage in this regard therefore:

- Non specialist lawyers should no longer be permitted to accept instructions in public law proceedings.

- Courts should have a duty to provide parents with lists of local Children Panel solicitors.

Instructing experts and future policy

A great deal of attention has focused on the problems involved in using experts in care proceedings since the Children Act 1989. There has been less attention comparing care proceedings under the preceding legislation and on identifying some of the current benefits.

Compared with the investigation processes and legal proceedings under previous legislation, under the Children Act, we are in fact "doing it better": more expertise is employed, more options are pursued, issues are made clearer earlier in the case, and all parties have access to the same information.

However, certain issues need clarification:

- The joint instruction of experts will not be appropriate or achievable in all cases.

- The existing body of child welfare knowledge is neither static nor uniform and consultants do not always necessarily agree with the local authority. On that basis and in the interests of social justice, legal procedures for the appointment of experts should not reduce the opportunities for that breadth of relevant knowledge to inform decision making with regard to the future care and wellbeing of very vulnerable children.

- It should be remembered that not all expert evidence will be highly contentious and likely to result in a fully contested final hearing. It should also be noted that not all reports filed in cases will have been based on assessments commissioned during the current proceedings. Some will be "prior" reports based on assessment undertaken before proceedings commenced.

It should also be noted that:

- Courts and guardians already have the power to exert control over the conduct of cases during the early stages. That potential could be more fully utilised but to be effective it must be done in conjunction with a move towards improving the quality of legal representation for parents.

Appendix 1 – Duration

The variables

Below, we outline the statistical exercise undertaken with four variables (with acronyms in brackets) in order to arrive at the findings outlined in Chapter 4. First, we explain each variable. We then explore the mean differences in duration for each of these four variables in order to see whether variation in the length of cases is associated with the different factors. Having established that, we then explored whether these different factors were acting independently of each other with regard to their impact on duration in cases. That exercise allowed us to arrive at the conclusion that, when all variables we considered are included in the model, whether a case was transferred between courts was the main explanation for increased duration.

1 Type of application (TYPEAPP)

Most applications included an application for a care order (82 per cent). Duration was compared between two groups of cases: those cases which contained an application for a care order and other types of applications (the latter were too few in number to be described separately).

2 Number of applications within a case (NAPP)

As we outlined above (Table 4.5) most applications were for a single order (92 per cent). Duration was compared between two groups of cases: those containing a single application and those containing two or more applications.

3 The court in which the current application started and whether it was transferred (TRANSFER)

Six mutually exclusive groups were identified in the sample:

– whether the case started and completed in a Family Proceedings Court or,

– was transferred from a Family Proceedings Court and completed in a Care Centre or,

– started in a Family Proceedings Court and finished in the High Court or,

– started and finished in a Care Centre or,

– started in a Care Centre and was transferred to the High Court or,

– started and finished in the High Court

4 Reports filed: the filing party, the number of parties filing and whether the case contained any reports based on joint instructions (INSTRUCT)

These factors were combined into the following (five) mutually exclusive groups:

– cases in which only the local authority instructed experts and filed reports

– cases in which only the guardian *ad litem* instructed experts and filed reports

– cases in which only the parent(s)/carers instructed experts and filed reports

– cases which contained a report based on a joint instruction

– cases in which more than one party instructed experts and filed reports

Table 7.1 gives the mean duration for these factors.

	Mean duration	95% confidence limits lower	upper	Number of cases
Whether case contained an application for a care order:				
Yes	9.17	8.08	10.26	95
No	8.14	7.74	8.55	445
Number of applications pertaining to case:				
One	8.15	7.76	8.54	498
Two or more	10.40	8.75	12.06	42
Start and final order court:				
FPC to FPC	6.36	5.95	6.77	190
CC to CC	7.52	6.19	8.86	40
FPC to CC	9.28	8.61	9.95	229
FPC to HC	10.80	9.68	11.93	61
CC to HC	11.00	1.91	20.09	4
HC to HC	9.75	7.69	11.81	16
Instructing party:				
Local authority only	6.87	6.37	7.38	142
Guardian only	8.00	7.01	8.99	91
Parent only	7.73	6.58	8.88	26
Multiple parties	9.38	8.73	10.04	250
Joint instructions	7.87	6.99	8.75	31

Table 7.1

Duration of cases (months) by explanatory variables

Variation in duration and relevant factors: mean differences

1 TYPEAPP – The mean difference in duration between those cases which included an application for a care order and the other group of cases is statistically significant ($p<0.05$). Those cases which included an application for a care order took an average of one month less to complete.

2 NAPP – The mean differences between those cases which were single applications and those where there were two or more applications is statistically significant ($p<0.01$). Single applications took an average of 2.25 months less to complete.

3 TRANSFER -The mean differences between the six groups that define the court in which the case started and whether it was transferred are also statistically significant ($p<0.001$).

4 INSTRUCT – The mean differences between cases based on the parties filing reports are also significant ($p<0.01$).

The mean differences in duration described in Table 7.1 were obtained from a random sample of cases and are thus sample estimates of duration in general. Table 7.1 also includes 95 per cent confidence intervals for these sample estimates and it can, for example, be seen that the estimated mean duration for cases which included a care application has a lower limit at 7.74 months and an upper limit at 8.55 months.

Variation in duration has thus been shown to be associated with the different factors.

Assessing relative impact on duration

The next question addressed was whether these factors are acting independently of each other with regard to their association with duration. Multiple regression analyses were undertaken.* The variables TYPEAPP and INSTRUCT are highly correlated and their effects on duration are difficult to disentangle. One analysis was therefore undertaken with variables TYPEAPP, NAPP and TRANSFER in a model and a further model with NAPP, TRANSFER, and INSTRUCT.

The multiple regression analyses showed that the Transfer variable was the most important in explaining the duration of cases. Type of Application and Instructing/Filing party were far less significant. The association between the Number of Applications and duration is explained away by these other variables.

Table 7.2 contains the results from the multiple regression analyses.† Cases which started in the Family Proceedings Court or started and completed in the Care Centre were used as the baseline group. Compared with the baseline group, cases which transferred from a Family Proceedings Court to a Care Centre took an extra 3 months to complete. Cases which transferred from a Family Proceedings Court through to the High Court took an extra 4.5 months to complete. Cases which either started in a Care Centre and transferred to the High court or, started and completed in the High Court took nearly 3 months longer to complete than the baseline group.

Cases where a care order was included in the application took an average of nearly 2 months less than a baseline group of all other cases. Cases which contained reports filed by more than one party (multiple parties filing) took an average of 1.2 months more than all other cases.

*The group of cases "started in the Care Centre and completed in the High Court" is combined with the group of cases "started and completed in the High Court" because of small numbers in the former – see Table 4.3).

† One analysis with the Transfer and Type of Application variables in the model and that for the Instructing/Filing party based on a model with Transfer and Instructing Parties present.

Table 7.2

Results of multiple regression analysis

Note: * It was not possible to include type of application and instructing party in the same model because of problems of collinearity. Results for transfer are included for the model containing type of applicaion and transfer.
** Baseline group consists of cases started and finished in the FPC or started and finished in the CC.
*** Baseline group consists of local authority only, guardian only, parent only, or joint instruction

	Duration change compared to baseline groups (months) (+ = more than baseline group – = less than baseline group)	95% confidence intervals (months)
Whether case contained an application for a care order compared to baseline group of no care order	–1.87	–2.85 to –0.89
*Start court and final order court compared with baseline group**		
FPC to CC	+3.03	2.24 to 3.83
FPC to HC	+4.56	3.36 to 5.77
CC to HC or all HC	+2.89	0.93 to 4.84
*Instructing party***	+1.20	0.45 to 1.95

Additional analyses undertaken

The results presented above have ignored the clustering of cases within individual guardians. They provided data on their two most recently completed cases and it may be that there is some association between duration and guardians which could not be revealed by ignoring the hierarchy of cases provided by guardians themselves.

In order to address this possibility, duration was also examined using multilevel modelling methods with cases at level 1 and guardians at level 2. The main effect analyses already described were also undertaken in a multilevel framework but they provided no evidence that variation in duration could be explained by the clustering (variation at level 2 never exceeded 4 per cent and never differed significantly from zero percent). Thus, the simpler single level analyses have been presented. In other words, we have looked at the possibility of an impact of the guardian hierarchy on duration and for the purposes of this sample we can ignore this aspect.

The statistical analyses undertaken demand that the variable being modelled (duration of cases) should roughly follow a Normal distribution. A simple log transformation of the duration resulted in a much better fit to the Normal distribution. Analyses were also undertaken on the transformed variable and the fit was better (adjusted r squared of 17 per cent against 14 per cent). The results of this analysis have not been presented as they are not as directly interpretable as the untransformed analysis presented. The transformed analyses differ marginally from the untransformed analyses but not in terms of variables being allowed to enter or leave the model.

Duration of cases – conclusion

The major finding when all variables are included in the model is that transfer is the main explanatory variable:

- The court where a case started and whether it was subsequently transferred was found to be the main explanation for duration.

- Cases containing applications for a care order were associated with a small decrease in duration which was independent of the start court or transfer status.

- Cases in which more than one party filed expert reports were found to be associated with a small increase in duration which was independent of start court or transfer status but not independent of whether the case contained an application for a care order.

There is, however, much variation which has not been explained by this modelling. It may be that there are other variables which would further explain variation in the duration of cases. For example, one important variable for further investigation would be the length of time cases wait for a first directions hearing following the date of transfer but for which we do not have data. It would also be important to look at whether cases were contested at the final hearing and if not, the point at which cases ceased to be contested. We know from existing data (Bates & Brophy, forthcoming) that in certain locations at least, the process of commissioning expert evidence usually starts at the beginning of cases (i.e. at the first directions hearing) but this may not be a national trend.

8

References

Barn R (1993) *Black Children in the Public Care System*, London: Batsford.

Bates P & Brophy J (1996) *The Appliance of Science?: Use of Experts in Care Proceedings – A Court-Based Study* (forthcoming).

Bebbington A & Miles J (1989) 'The Background of Children Who Enter Local Authority Care', *British Journal of Social Work*, Vol 19, pp 349–368.

Booth Dame Margaret (1996) *Avoiding Delay in Children Act Cases*, London: Lord Chancellor's Department.

Brophy J & Bates P (1998) 'The Position of Parents Using Experts in Care Proceedings – A Failure of "Partnership"?' *The Journal of Social Welfare and Family Law*, Vol 20, No 1 pp 21–48.

Brophy J, Wale C J & Bates P (1997) Training and Support: The Guardian ad Litem and Reporting officer Service, DoH/Welsh Office/Thomas Coram Research Unit, Institute of Education, University of London.

Brophy J, Brown L, Cohen S & Radcliffe P (1997) Law and 'Medicine' Psychiatry at the Interface of Child Protection Litigation, Report prepared for the Department of Health.

Brophy J & Bates P (1999) The Guardian *ad Litem*: Complex Cases and the Use of Experts following the 1989 Children Act, London: Lord Chancellor's Department.

Children Act Advisory Committee, The (1996) *Annual Report 1994/95*, London: Lord Chancellor's Department.

Children Act Advisory Committee, The (1995) *Annual Report 1993/94*, London: Lord Chancellor's Department.

Children Act Advisory Committee, The (1994) *Annual Report 1992/93*, London: Lord Chancellor's Department.

Children Act Advisory Committee, The (1993) *Annual Report 1991/92*, London: Lord Chancellor's Department.

Department of Health (SSI) (1995) *The Challenge of Partnership in Child Protection: Practice Guide*, London: HMSO.

Department of Health, Social Services Inspectorate (1995) *The Guardian Ad Litem & Reporting Officer Service. Annual Reports 1994–1995: An Overview*, London: Department of Health.

Department of Health (1994) *The Guardian Ad Litem & Reporting Officer Service. Annual Reports: 1993–1994*, London: Department of Health.

Department of Health (1991a) *The Children Act 1989, Guidance and Regulations: Vol 1, Court Orders*, London: HMSO.

Department of Health (1991b) *The Children Act 1989, Guidance and Regulations: Vol 2, Family Support, Day care and Educational provision for Young Children*, London: HMSO.

Department of Health (1991c) *The Children Act 1989, Guidance and Regulations: Vol 3, Family Placements*, London: HMSO

Department of Health (1988) *Protecting Children: A Guide for Social Workers Undertaking a Comprehensive Assessment*, London: HMSO.

Expert Witness Group (1997) Bristol: Family Law.

Foster B & Preston-Shoot, M (1995) *Guardians ad Litem and Independent Expert Assessments*, School of Social Work, University of Manchester.

Home Office, Department of Health, Department of Education & Science, Welsh Office. (1991) *Working Together. A guide to arrangements for inter-agency co-operation for the protection of children from abuse*, London: HMSO.

Hunt J (1993) *Local Authority Wardships before the Children Act, The Baby or the Bathwater*, London: HMSO

Independent Representation for Children in Need (IRCHIN) (1994) *Practice in Progress 1994. The A-Z of Care Management: A National Report*, Independent Representation for Children in Need/Department of Health.

James A (1992) 'An Open or Shut Case? Law as an Autopoietic System', *Journal of Law & Society*, Vol 19, No 2, pp 272–283.

King M (1991) 'Children and the Legal Process: Views from a Mental Health Clinic'. *Journal of Social Welfare Law*, No 4, pp 269–284.

King M & Trowell, J (1992) *Children's Welfare and the Law: The Limits of Legal Intervention*, London: Sage.

Law Society, The (1996), *Directory of Expert Witnesses*. London: Law Society

Millham S, Bullock R, Hosie K & Haak M (1986) *Lost in Care: The problems of maintaining links between children in care and their families*, Hants: Gower.

OPCS/GRO(S) (1994) 1991 *Census: Ethnic Group and Country of Birth, Great Britain*, London: HMSO.

Packman J (1986) *Child Care: Needs and Numbers*. London: Allen & Unwin.

Packman J, Randal, J & Jacques, N (1986) *Who Needs Care?* Oxford: Blackwell.

Phoenix A & Owen C (1996) 'From Miscegenation to Hybridity: mixed relationships and mixed parentage in profile', pp 111–135 in, Brannen J & Bernstein B (eds) *Children, Research and Policy: Essays for Barbara Tizard*, London: Taylor & Francis.

Plotnikoff J & Woolfson R (1994) *The Children Act 1989: Timetabling of Interim Care Orders Study*, London: SSI, Department of Health.

Sackett V L, Rosenberg W M C, Muir Gray J A, Haynes P B, and Richardson W S (1996) 'Evidence based medicine: What it is and what it isn't.' *British Medical Journal*, Vol 512, 71–72.

Sepping P (1992) 'A Future for Children's Health Services'. *Panel News, Independent Representation for Children in Need*, Vol 5, No 4, pp 23–25.

Thoburn J, Lewis A & Shemmings D (1995) 'Family Participation in Child Protection', *Child Abuse Review*, Vol 4, pp161–171.

Trowell J (1991) 'What is Happening to Mental Health Services for Children and Young People and Families'. *Association of Child Psychology and Psychiatry, Review and Newsletter*, Vol 13, No 5, pp 12–15.

Tunnard J (1991) 'Setting the Scene for Partnership', in Tunnard J (ed), *The Children Act, Working in Partnerhsip with Families: A Reader*, London: HMSO, pp 1–6.

Wall The Hon Mr Justice (1995) *The Use or Misuse of Experts – When and Who to Instruct.* Conference Paper, National Conference: The National Association of Guardians *ad Litem* and Reporting Officers, Bath.

Wolkind S (1994) *The Challenge of Expert Opinion*. Conference Paper, British Juvenile & Family Court Society/Institute of Psychiatry, March, London.